If Money Could Talk

By George A. McConechy, CFP®, FMA®, PFP®, CIWM®, FCSI®

About the Author

George McConechy

When I began my career as an Investment Advisor in 2001, I did it with the philosophy that health and happiness are the focal point of a life well lived. Money is simply a tool that enables my clients live the life they deserve — both today and in the future.

I believe in following a sensible approach to money management with a 360-degree view of the entire picture. It sounds simple, but patience and a practical approach have led to far richer rewards than the latest investment fad, or chasing an elusive rate of return.

My goal is to become the "go-to" resource on all things related to money. In addition to keeping my finger on the pulse of what matters most to clients and what role money can play in a lifetime, I've focused on continuous learning. I've earned designations as a Certified Financial Planner (CFP), Financial Management Advisor (FMA), Certified International Wealth Manager (CIWM), Personal Financial Planner (PFP) and earned my fellowship of the Canadian Securities Institute (FCSI).

But no matter how many certificates may hang on my wall, I will never forget that success in the investment industry comes from three things: an ability to focus on the client, see the solutions with clarity, and deliver results with commitment.

Foreword

Scott McCartney

In 2013, I entered into a professional financial partnership with George McConechy. We had the idea that together, we can take our clients on a unique journey.

The big questions were "How could we make a significant impact on each client's unique financial situation?" What did "Wealth Management" mean to us? How were we going to make that "significant impact"? What process could we use to deliver a truly world class wealth management experience for our clients?

For us, Wealth Management must address the major concerns that successful individuals, families and business owners share: Investment Counselling, Wealth Enhancement, Wealth Transfer, Wealth Protection and Charitable Planning.

By joining forces and engaging the expertise of other professionals, George and I are able to cohesively deliver wealth management solutions to our clients, delivering the financial peace of mind that our clients are aiming for.

☙

Contents

Retirement. It Takes Practice. 1

Spending Your Way to Happiness 13

Taking Care of Business 23

Filling Your Retirement Bucket.. 33

One tickbox can change your life... 41

The Golden Handshake.. 45

The Bucket System for Retirement 49

Your Home is Your Castle.. 55

A Blizzard for Snowbirds 59

'Til Death Do Us Part 65

How To Screw Up Your Estate Plan With One Signature 76

'Til Divorce Do Us Part.. 81

Dependent Adults.. 89

The Peanut Butter Generation 99

Leaving a Legacy 105

Protect Your Earning Power 117

Your Relationship with Money... 124

Choosing a Financial Advisor Isn't Easy 134

Don't Worry. Be Happy.. 143

Index.. 145

Introduction

Whether or not you've followed the script all your life about saving for retirement, paying yourself first and taking care of the future, there comes a point when you realize: 'Holy cow. Retirement is closer than I thought.'

And if you're like most Canadians, after age 50 you'll discover the road is a lot more crooked than it looked. There are aging parents, divorces, blended families, market meltdowns, children who don't leave home (or who come back with babies in tow), health challenges, real estate mistakes, golden handshakes, business opportunities — just to name a few — that have entered the mix and left you wondering just what exactly you're supposed to do next.

Since 2001 I've been advising Canadians on the straightest path to prosperity and I've discovered that most books about money are about just that — money. And that there isn't really a book about life and how money fits into it. That's why I decided to write one.

People have an unusual relationship with money. It's not about what makes you feel good because money has no feeling. It has no personality. Money is a commodity. Money works for you. Money is your employee. Some of my views on money might clash with your gut feelings, but I'm hopeful that while you're reading, you're able to think about it with your mind only and leave your stomach out of it.

I've organized the book by what might be happening in your life and how you can handle the money decisions that impact it. Therefore if you've not experienced divorce, there's probably no need to read that chapter. Feel free to graze for the topics that mean the most to you. And hopefully you won't recognize yourself or your loved ones in the tales of regret that I've sprinkled throughout.

The long and the short of it is that somewhere before or after the age of 50, life gets complicated. And you'll need professional advice to tease out the good decisions from the bad when all things — relative to you — are considered.

And while we're on the topic of advice, I urge you to seek the best advice from the most experienced advisors. Your tax accountant should be good at taxes. Your divorce lawyer should be good at family law. But your divorce lawyer shouldn't be the one you turn to when you're valuing your business, and your tax accountant might not be the best choice to help you with setting up a trust for your disabled child. They'll do their best — there's no doubt about that. But sometimes it takes a specialist with in-depth knowledge on that particular subject to make sure that you've ticked the right boxes, paid the least taxes and given your heirs the fewest headaches or whatever else is important to you.

George

Retirement. It Takes Practice.

People often ask if me if they can afford to retire at age 55. But the answer I always have to give is 'that depends'. It depends on three things: 1) How long you're planning to live; 2) What you want to do in retirement; and 3) Where you want to live.

The Wild Card

In 2001, Statistics Canada decided for the first time to count the number of people over age 100. There were 3,400. In 2006, there were 6,000. According to the latest population projections, the number of centenarians could reach 15,000 by 2030[1]. By the way, that's not your children turning 100 in 2030. It's your parents! 2030 is much closer than we think—it's today's 80 year-olds.

According to Statistics Canada, a child born today has a life expectancy of 78 for

Canadian Life Expectancy

	Male	Female
At birth	78	83
Age 50	80	84
Age 65	83	86
Age 80	88	90

---

1 http://publications.gc.ca/Collection/Statcan/96F0030X/96F0030XIE2001002.pdf

men and 83[2] for women. If you've already made it to age 50, your odds are more along the lines of living to 80 for men and 84 for women because the formula leaves out all of the people who've already died before you — from infant mortality, teenage misadventures, congenital diseases, etc.

At age 50 you haven't gained much ground in the life expectancy sweepstakes. As you move into later years, you gain ground more rapidly as those who have passed on from early cancer or accidents have already been removed. At age 65, a male is expected to survive another 18 years, to about age 83, and a female almost 21 more years, to about age 86.

Of course, you can't count on living as long as the tables say, but it's also a mistake to plan your retirement around the idea that you're going to die in your 70s. The tables are based on the broad population, including smokers and non-smokers, marathoners and couch potatoes, and people with all sorts of good and bad family genes. You'll get a more realistic picture if you adjust what you read in the tables based on knowledge of your own factors.

So the first part of my answer is always that you can't afford to lose sight of the fact that you may require a retirement 'paycheque' for 40 years or more and that definitely may change your idea of whether you retire at 55, 65 or 75.

And here's another plain fact: You may actually miss working. Even if you have abundant income and assets to support yourself in retirement, you may regret

Playing the Odds

You have to allow for good or bad luck. Some people plan to run out of money when they die, but forget to die on schedule. Make sure your needs will be covered even if you live longer than the life expectancy tables say you should.

❖

2 http://www5.statcan.gc.ca/cansim/a26

giving up the daily routine and camaraderie of a job.

Oddly enough, all our working years, we wish for freedom. We can't wait for the day we walk out the proverbial retirement door. And yet, many people find it isn't what they expected. I've had numerous clients who retired and then went back to work for reasons that had nothing to do with money.

If the only thing you wake up to each morning in retirement is your spouse or significant other, you might find yourself a little 'out of sorts'. Even if your sweetie — suffering from too much togetherness — doesn't end up killing you, retirement itself just might.

Retirement Syndrome

We've all heard stories of guys who, after busting their hump for 40 years, kick the bucket a few months before or after their retirement party. These stories scare the crap out of me and make me wonder about the idea of retirement, or on the flip side, working so hard to accomplish retirement.

Bored to Death?

Suddenly all this free time with no commitments! But does that make you happy, or anxious? After all, what happens when we retire? For many, a whole lot of nothing. Maybe some games of bridge, golf, and lying on the beach, but doesn't that get boring? Yes, and in fact, it might even bore you to death!

A study published in the British Medical Journal in 2010 found that people who retired at 55 were almost twice as likely to die within 10 years after retirement as those who stuck it out at work until 65[3].

---

3 http://longevity.about.com/od/healthyagingandlongevity/a/retirement.htm

After accounting for ill health and other variables, the only difference between the two groups was retirement from work. From this, experts infer that work could be the reason we continue to live as long as we do — because it gives us purpose.

Replacing Your Purpose

Many people who leave work aren't really sure what to do with their days. One of my clients at age 50 can relate; one of the worst years of her life was when she was unemployed — not because she didn't know where the money was coming from (she had a three-year severance package) but because she didn't have anything that would fill her days with meaning. The lesson she learned early is that even if you're financially free, it doesn't mean you'll be living a fulfilling life.

Without a purpose people tend to live shorter lives.

Sounds a bit morbid, but it's true. Dan Buettner is a world-renowned explorer and a writer for National Geographic. He travels the world speaking at seminars and on TV, sharing the habits that lead to long life. He is the founder of Quest Network. When he discussed his interviews with centenarians at a TED presentation[4] he found that they were all able to tell him exactly what their purpose was. Ironic? I doubt it.

If your purpose is your work, you will need to find another purpose before you set sail into retirement. It's something to be considered long and hard. You don't want to be arguing with your sweetie about whose turn it is to do the vacuuming, or which brand of spaghetti sauce has the greatest merits. One final tip

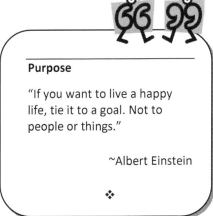

Purpose

"If you want to live a happy life, tie it to a goal. Not to people or things."

~Albert Einstein

❖

---

4 http://www.ted.com/talks/dan_buettner_how_to_live_to_be_100.html

from those who have successfully retired: 'travel' is not purpose. 'Golf' is not purpose. Those are diversions for which you will now have more time, but they are not purpose.

I can't begin to help my clients find their purpose, but I have seen some great examples: writing books, consulting, playing an active role in grandchildren's lives, working on international relief efforts, the Seniors' Olympics, university educations, opening a business, volunteer work — the sky's the limit.

A Door Closes. A Door Opens.

The hard part about retirement — whether you believe it or not — is closing the door on who you were. For almost 40 years, you've spent a third of your day at your workplace, if not more. If you're a business owner, it's usually way more. It becomes your life and you really have to get your head wrapped around the fact that when you retire, that person is gone. And for many professionals, it also means giving up your identity. You no longer get to introduce yourself as 'Judy, the Vice President of Marketing'. You're 'Just Judy'.

You're giving up all those people you see on a day-to-day basis: the security guard, the mailman, the receptionist, the people you meet in the elevator or the ones in the car park, whatever. It is going to be a mental shift in order to be comfortable with where you're going. And the future has to look as interesting as the past. Otherwise you'll be one of those old farts who live in the past and never let a chance to reminisce go by without a long tangent.

The Other Big Questions

Where will you live?

I've heard that Nova Scotia is really inexpensive but is that where you want to live? Do you want to stay where you are? Move nearer to family? (Or further away?) Move to something smaller? Do you want a house in Palm Beach? A pied-à-terre in Provence?

It's time to think about those things now. Life between 50 and 60 just zings by. And as you get older, the pages flip faster and faster.

There used to be an old crock about retirement that you would be able to live on a third of your working income. That's probably a holdover from the days when life expectancy was 49 and retirement age was 65. Chances are your expenses before retirement and after retirement aren't going to change very much, if any. In the early years of retirement, they may even go up.

How will you spend your time?

This is a bit of a continuation on the subject of purpose. If golf is your passion, you can't golf 365 days a year — at least not in Canada. And you can't golf 12 hours a day, at least not every day. Will you volunteer? Go back to university? All these things add to your costs and you'll need to make sure you have the cash in hand.

What big obligations do you have?

If you're going into retirement with consumer debt and mortgages, they're not going to vanish. If you need to purchase an RV or new cars, your advisor will need to help you make sure the funds are liquid and ready to roll when you are. Of course, if you've still got kids in the nest, or aging parents to parent, there are other considerations to debate.

It Takes Some Thought

Most people spend less time planning their retirement than choosing a new car. And worse, some spend more time picking their numbers for lotto. I know it's sad, but that's just one of those little quirky things that you find out as an advisor.

❖

Got the Travel Bug?

Most people haven't really thought about what they want to do in their retirement. I often hear 'travel', 'golf', 'head south' or even just as simple as 'not go to work'.

It's very difficult to plan for a retirement when the picture isn't clear. For example: travel where? How? There's a big difference between making gruel on an eco-project in Costa Rica and dining at the Tour d'Argent in France. A big difference between motorcycling with a backpack across the country and rolling down the highway in the latest Winnebago with a satellite dish on top and a car in tow.

If the travel bug is in your future, start to make a list today of where exactly you'd like to go, how you'd like to get there and what you want to do while you're there. Get on the computer. Google is your friend! Write it down — Australian outback, African safari, castles of Europe — do your research and get a rough idea of how much money you're going to need to get there. You don't need to break it down into a daily budget, but if you can pin it down to an annual ballpark, you can plan for it that much easier.

Be Careful What You Ask For

So let's say the idea of being a 'snowbird' has a certain appeal. Your retirement approaches and you buy a condo in Belize or someplace else tropical. You quit your job, you sell your house, leave your friends and family behind for the beauty of a beach in Belize. In fact, you've just completely and totally uprooted your life. On more than one occasion, I've seen people do that and realize after one year, or maybe two, that they hate it. They miss their friends, their social life, their family (and maybe even their work).

Retirement is just like everything else. If you're trying a new food, you don't just take a great big spoon of it and stick it in your mouth. You take a little taste before you take a big bite.

Another example from my clients: winterizing the cottage so that they can live there year-round. The cottage is so full of happy, relaxing memories. But winter in cottage country can be a lot like winter on the moon. One of my clients said, "You don't know silence, until you've heard -40°C silence on a frozen lake." Imagine 4 months without friends, restaurants, movie theatres, or even traffic. If that's the solitude you crave, then awesome. But for my client, retirement at the cottage was an unexpected bore.

Advertising vs Reality

A 2011 poll conducted by RBC[5] shows us that what we think we want to do and what we end up really doing in retirement appears to be different. The poll focused on the expectations of near retirees versus those already retired. Some of the interesting results include:

- nearly 75% of Canadians over 50 think they'll spend retirement days travelling but only 58% of those retired spend time away from home;
- 30% of those nearly retired or over 50 believe they will spend winters down south and summers in Canada — the snowbird lifestyle — but only 14% of those retired live the snowbird lifestyle;
- 60% of women near retirement expect to do volunteer work once retired but 41% actually do;
- 53% of men near retirement expect to do volunteer work once retired but 35% actually do;

The key takeaway is not to box yourself in. Working through your retirement expectations and trying things on for size are important exercises. The sooner done the better!

---

[5] http://www.rbc.com/newsroom/2011/0420-myths-wave1.html

The long and short of it is to take your retirement plans on a test drive. Go for an extended vacation before you make a permanent decision. Go alone, without family or friends. Doing it for real is a huge mental shift from doing it as a 2-week vacation away from work. You'll get a taste, smell and feel for what it's like, before you pull the retirement pin. And you'll get a sense of just how much it's going to cost. This is, of course, extremely helpful in setting up your retirement income flow.

So even with all of that said, I'm certain that I haven't scared you away from the idea of retirement. So my only goal is to help you plan for it, practice it and ultimately enjoy it.

So How Much Do You Need?

Just like your needs, activities and expenses have evolved over the last 40 years, the next 40 years will not be all homogenous. It's important to think of retirement in phases. You're not going to spend the same money throughout all the different phases of retirement. So you can spend more at first, and rely on different places or different income buckets throughout retirement.

The go-go phase.

The go-go phase is the first retirement phase when we tend to be physically and mentally capable of living fairly active lives. For some, the active phase will include work. It may be part-time work or consulting in the same field as your pre-retirement career, or it may mean self-employment. And as I've mentioned, it's not work for the money, but work for the purpose — the meaning and the social life. Sure there will be some golf mixed in. Some travel. Some prolonged respite from the cold Canadian winters, but in all, there will be purpose.

Whatever the case, active retirement is really living the stereotypical retirement dream. For many retirees in this phase, they are busier than they were before they retired as they squeeze as much pleasure and enjoyment out of their freedom as possible.

Do You Still Need a Cushion?

All through your earning years, your advisor has preached the virtues of having a financial cushion — a liquid sum that can be accessed for emergencies. The bad news: Emergencies still happen when you're retired. The furnace could still break. All the shingles can blow off the roof or wear out. You might need a new car or your adult children may need to be bailed out of jail [you never know!]. Add to that the thrill of spontaneity in retirement. If your friends invite you to join them on a cruise up the Mekong River in Cambodia, you may want to go along since friendship and companionship are what life is all about. You're free, you're financially able, so don't let a lack of liquidity spoil your spontaneity.

The slow-go phase.

The next phase of retirement is the slow-go phase where the body is telling you to slow down. Between the ages of 70 and 84, life starts falling into patterns and becoming more stable.

You probably know people in this phase. They have very predictable routines: banking on Mondays, groceries on Wednesdays, bridge on Fridays. One reason is that energy levels are changing and patterns help minimize effort and thought without compromising on the enjoyment of life. By the age of 75-85, many people quit traveling. They'll just drive or go to places that are within a day or two of home. Travel health insurance becomes unaffordable, so staying within Canada is the norm.

The no-go phase.

The last phase in retirement is the no-go phase or the limited retirement phase. While we all hope to die in our sleep after a great round of golf, the more realistic picture is that our choices become much more limited by health and ability. This unfortunately doesn't mean that this phase of retirement is 'cheap'. Often this stage requires some level of support from family, governments or agencies, whether it's assisted living, nursing homes or home care or even just help with the lawn, the pool maintenance or housework. And if you don't want your children choosing your nursing home, you'll want to make sure that this phase of retirement is adequately funded from your retirement bucket of savings.

If all goes according to Hoyle, you'll probably need more income in the go-go phase of retirement and slow down the older you get. But make no mistake about it, the third phase of retirement can be the most costly of all and that's one risk you can't afford to ignore when you're setting up your retirement income bucket system.

$traight Talk

Make lists. What you'd like to do. Where you'd like to go. Check out how much it's going to cost.

It's time to start trying things on for size. Does it suit you to be a snowbird? Do you really enjoy living out of a suitcase? Can you really golf 18 holes a day for days on end? Do you like being away from family and friends? Can you and your partner / spouse / significant other stand that much togetherness?

Unless you've already received news to the contrary, there's a great chance you'll live well past 80. It's better to count on that, than to run out of money before you run out of days.

Spending Your Way to Happiness

Take everything you've ever heard about money and put it aside. No matter what kind of career you've had, whether you're great at picking stocks or have just socked money away under the mattress for years, there are some basic good habits that will garner you a rich retirement. Even if you've ignored these simple habits up until now, there's still time to change your ways and make an impact on your retirement.

Know Your Numbers

Let's suppose you're not a big fan of budgets and the thought of denying yourself that shiny new tool for your garage (or passing up a deal on that Gucci bag) makes you feel like you're living in a prison. Of course you're not alone. But there are some basic numbers that I make sure that my clients know off by heart.

What is an hour of your time really worth?

Take your gross annual salary, minus taxes and CPP and anything else that is deducted before you see the cheque. Divide it by 48 or 50 weeks (however many weeks a year you work). Then divide that by 37.5. That's the value of an hour. Now you'll know exactly how many hours that shiny new tool is worth. Or that Gucci bag. Or even that iced latte on Sunday morning. It feels very different to make your spending decisions knowing exactly how long it takes to make that kind of money.

What does it take to run the ship?

By that I mean you need to know all of your fixed costs — the things you can't control. Add up the mortgage, insurance, property tax, telephone, cable TV, electricity, heat, water and any other essentials for your existence. Those are your fixed costs. And now that you know how much an hour of your time is worth, you'll know exactly how many hours it takes you each month to just keep the ship afloat.

If you don't like what you learn, make adjustments.

I'm never one to say what's essential in life and what isn't. But if you don't like the number of hours it takes to keep the ship afloat, make some decisions. If you'd like to have more discretionary income to play with, there are choices to be made there too.

Good Debts vs Bad Debts

Credit cards are not just bad debt. They're evil debt. They're the reason banks are such a great equity investment — they're very profitable. Car loans, higher interest rate loans and in-store financing loans are all what we call 'bad debts'. Bad debt is when you borrow to purchase something that you either consume quickly or decreases in value over time. People use credit cards to pay for vacations, meals and other consumable products. These products soon lose their value, and the effect of continued interest rates on the unpaid credit-card balance causes the price of these already-gone products to keep going up and up.

Of course credit cards can be a great convenience, as long as you are disciplined enough to pay the balance in full each month. If you're not that disciplined, my advice is always to use cash. Even your debit card doesn't give you the same sensation as peeling off a wad of $20 bills to pay for that facial or that new golf club.

For those of us who grew up with parents who lived through the depression, there's an old mantra that all debt is bad, but believe it or not, some debt can be ok... maybe even good. For example:

- a debt that you use to purchase an asset that will appreciate in value or can be sold at a profit like a home or an investment;

- a debt that you use to purchase something like a business or a rental property. If you buy something that pays an income, you can use that income to pay off the debt;

- a debt for something that will improve your quality of life like a student loan, medical supplies, home renovations to improve handicapped access etc.

Money in Your Wallet

I used to assume that by the time a couple hit age 50, their ability to handle the responsibility of credit cards was a given. Clearly the television shows about getting out of debt have proven me wrong. The biggest mistake many couples make is carrying too much debt. And once the debt burden gets heavier, it gets harder and harder to crawl out from under it. It's one thing to spend freely when you're young and single. But add car payments, mortgages, boats, snowmobiles and winter vacations to the equation, and everything changes.

Adding fuel to the fire is the seemingly benign offer to "open a store's credit card account today and receive 20% off the cost of your purchase". The only way that makes sense is if you'll pay the balance in full. Otherwise the 'savings' will be destroyed by the high interest rate on the card.

The Beauty of Cash

If you become accustomed to using cash, you'll make much better spending decisions. When you actually have to pull out the cash to pay, you may in fact decide it's not worth it. Because earning money is tough. If you're making $50 an hour and those shoes are $250, they'll take about 10 hours to earn because you have to pay for them with after tax dollars.

❖

There's an old adage that says: if you're going to buy something that doesn't go up in value — and you can't afford to pay cash (or use your debit card) — then you can't afford it. That general rule should be applied to all discretionary spending.

Here's a six-pack on what to do with those credit cards if they're calling out your name every time you leave home:

- Cut up all the ones that are usable at one place only — department store, gas station, hardware store. They most likely have the highest interest rates. Spreading the debt around can make you lose sight of just how much debt you've piled on;

- Pay attention to the credit card's interest rate and compare it to the cost of a bank loan. If you are carrying a debt from unpaid balances, you're likely better off getting a loan to pay off the cards. (And then stop using the cards!)

- Beware of the 'sale price' trap. If you're buying it because it's on sale (and you don't have the cash to pay the bill when it comes) it's not really on sale once the interest starts piling on;

- If you can't avoid the temptation when you're shopping, leave your credit card at home or at least in your trunk;

- Treat your credit card like an emergency safety net. If you have to use your credit card, revisit your numbers, cut back on nonessential spending and do anything you possibly can to bring your balance down to zero as soon as possible;

- Just say NO next time someone asks you if you'd like to apply for a credit card. If you've got one, you've got enough!

One final word on credit cards. Just because the bank says you qualify for another credit card, it doesn't mean you should apply. Remember that getting credit is one thing. Treating it responsibly is quite another.

Funding Your Mid-Life Crisis

If you're in the throes of a mid-life crisis and feel the need to buy a little sports coupe, take a sabbatical in the jungle or take your PhD in philosophy, there are ways to scratch that itch without taking a shovel to your retirement bucket.

If you're still working and paying taxes, you should almost NEVER think about tapping into your RRSP. The straight fact is that any time you withdraw from an RRSP it counts as income for that year. So if you are employed and you pull from an RRSP, your income goes up and you will pay more tax. The government always wants their money back. The only situation in life where it might make sense to tap into an RRSP would be to ward off bankruptcy.

Money Has No Feelings

Oddly enough, most peoople are far more emotionally attached to their home than their RRSP. They fear that tapping into their home as a source of cash is somehow taboo. Yet your home actually represents a much more practical source of money than an RRSP. If you own your home and you have some equity in it, it truly is the cheapest way to get money. You can do it through a mortgage (with a 30 year pay-back timetable) or through a secured line of credit, which might mean you don't need to pay it off even regularly if you need the breathing room.

If you're looking at a $100 bill, who cares whether it came from your house or from your RRSP? Only the tax man will know the difference. Your house will not.

If I haven't convinced you to keep your hands off your RRSP, let's take a practical example. Let's say you have your eye on a modest, used sports coupe that costs $21,000. (And you're earning $40,000 a year). If you've decided to tap into your RRSP, the first thing you'll have to do is withdraw $30,000 from your RRSP and send $9,000 withholding tax to the federal government instantly, so that you still have $21,000 to spend on that little shiny coupe. It's a bitter pill to swallow up front. But the cost doesn't stop there.

Borrowing to boost your RRSP

"Don't have the cash for an RRSP contribution? No problem. We'll lend you the money!" You can hear that offer every February. I am not a big fan of borrowing money to put it in your RRSP unless you've had an unusually large earning year and you want to shelter some of that extra income from tax.

My simple rule is two-fold. If you can't pay the whole loan back within one year, don't do it. And if you can't afford the loan repayment, don't do it. The worst possible situation is if you have to pull the money back out of the RRSP; you'll not only pay the tax, but you'll lose the contribution room forever.

Borrowing to invest makes sense in the long term only if the rate of return exceeds the interest rate on the loan. Obviously, it doesn't make sense to borrow at five per cent to invest in a term deposit making only 2 per cent! Once again, this strategy plays directly into the hands of those people who make a living off your money.

If you're in doubt, get someone to crunch the numbers for you. (And it likely shouldn't be the banker who will get compensated for getting your signature on the loan agreement.)

How a $21,000 Spending Spree Costs $72,000

If you had left it alone in your RRSP, that $30,000 would have grown to $72,000 over 15 years (assuming a 6% return), which might account for almost two years of living expenses in retirement. That's $42,000 robbed from your retirement bucket.

Fast forward by 15 years and that shiny sport coupe is a distant memory and worth absolutely squat. So the grand tally is as follows:

Car cost	$21,000
Withholding Taxes	$9,000
Opportunity Cost	$42,000
Total Cost	$72,000

And not to put too fine a point on it, but once you take the money out of the RRSP, you can't put it back. The contribution room is lost forever.

Hands Off that Tax Refund

I have come across so many unhealthy habits involving tax refunds that I almost dedicated an entire chapter to it.

First, let me say that I never advocate that my clients should live a parsimonious lifestyle. After all, money is a tool to be used and when used wisely can create a lifetime of enjoyment. What I do preach is that my clients should keep their hands off the tax refund cheque. It is not a windfall. It is your own money that the government has just been keeping for you for a short time.

If you're thinking about a winter vacation, a bathroom reno or a giant screen TV, it's far wiser to fund those from your regular income and not with your tax refund. Here are four far more practical ways to put that refund to use.

Free Up Short-Term Cash

If you normally carry a balance on your credit card (see above on bad debt) the highest and best use of your tax refund is to pay off the balance. The monthly interest savings alone can save you hundreds or thousands of dollars over the coming year and free-up your cash to invest in next year's RRSP.

Free Up Future Cash

Many mortgages allow you to make extra mortgage payments during the year. These extra payments go directly to reduce the principal. For example, let's assume you invested $10,000 in your RRSP this year and you are in a 40% marginal tax rate. You should save $4,000 in taxes and get that back in a refund. If you apply the refund to the mortgage, you have created $14,000 in wealth from a $10,000 contribution. Now for the bonus: the impact on your mortgage is even

How Fast Does $10,000 Grow?				
Yrs	4%	6%	8%	10%
10	$14,810	$17,910	$21,590	$29,940
20	$21,910	$32,070	$46,610	$67,280
30	$32,430	$57,430	$100,630	$174,409

❖

greater. Let's say your mortgage is $100,000 with a 25-year term and a 5% interest rate. A $4,000 prepayment will shave almost two years off the amortization and cut $8,500 in interest from your repayment cost. Imagine the possibilities if you made those same two transactions every year!

Pay Yourself Forward

The single-best strategy in order to pay yourself forward is to pump the refund straight into next year's RRSP contribution. It's like a chain reaction. Your RRSP contribution creates a tax refund, which creates an RRSP contribution, which creates a tax refund, etc. Here's a quick example on how to turn $10,000 into $16,500. Say you contribute $10,000 to an RRSP this year (year 1), and you receive a $4,000 tax refund in April next year (year 2):

- The $4,000 tax refund becomes your Year 2 RRSP contribution;

- In April of Year 3, that $4,000 RRSP contribution generates a new tax refund of $1,600;

- The $1,600 becomes your Year 4 RRSP contribution, which triggers a $640 tax refund in Year 5;

- That $640 becomes your Year 5 RRSP contribution and you get a $256 tax refund in Year 6.

Of course the refund gets smaller each year, but all the while, the original $10,000 is still growing (without tax) as well as each refund / contribution you've channeled back into it.

Think how much better it gets if you put in a new $10,000 each and every year (or whatever the maximum amount you're allowed). Each additional contribution sets up a new chain reaction on top of the earlier contributions.

Pay It Forward For Others

If you've been religious about maximizing your RSP contribution, there are still other ways to apply that refund to accumulate wealth. For example, a Registered Education Savings Plan (RESP) or Registered Disability Savings Plan (RDSP) are two ways that can bring matching government grants to boost your wealth and pay it forward to another family member.

Spending Spree

I think it's fairly obvious that you can't spend your way to happiness. If you can't pay for something with your 'day-job', you probably can't afford it. But most importantly, if you can resist the temptation to spend your tax refund on 'stuff' that doesn't improve your net worth, you'll be paying yourself forward (and forward and forward).

$traight Talk

Know Your Numbers: the value of an hour of your time and how much it takes to run your household ship so that you can weigh discretionary spending against something very concrete.

Resist the temptation to borrow money for things that don't add to your net worth or improve your quality of life.

Use your tax refund wisely. It's not a windfall; it's your own money.

Taking Care of Business

I have never met a business owner whose work day starts at 9 and ends at 5.

If you started your business in your thirties, you might look around you and realize that everybody you know is part of your business. All of the events you attend, the friends you have made are all connected in some way with your business. You are the business and the business is you. But what if you want to retire some day? How do you retire some day? Even if you're still on 'full battleship alert' and enjoying every minute of your business, do you think there might come a time when you want to slow down, pull back or ease up somewhat? Or is it your plan to die with your boots on? (There are some who decide to go that route!)

No matter what timeline you're looking at, you need an exit strategy — a way to transfer the business to family members, to sell the business to a buyer or some other creative solution to fund a retirement lifestyle.

There are consulting firms that can help you to find a buyer for your business. Finding a buyer is not the hard part, believe it or not. The hard part is figuring out what comes next. You can't just stop work, sit down on the easy chair at home and wash your hands of it.

Life After Work

There used to be an advertisement for a major Canadian mutual fund company that showed Spiderman on the golf course. And the slogan was something along the lines of "everyone has to retire someday..." Nothing could be truer for the business owner. Sure the first month or two might be full of travel, golf, sailing or whatever passions you've ignored during your business years. But then what?

And what about your friends who are still part of the business? What will you do — not just for money but what will you do with your time?

Long before you sell the business, it's really important to figure out how you're going to exit not only from the day-to-day running of the business, but exit from the community, the industry, and the clients. Some find it through consulting on a part time basis. Others have slowly exited by mentoring the person who takes over the business, or becoming an employee of the new owners throughout a transition period.

The short story is: regardless of whether you're planning to transfer the business to a family member, sell to a partner, management team or employees, or even sell to a third party, you'll need a mental and emotional exit strategy, not just a financial one.

Are you ready to sell?

If you've ever entertained thoughts of 'life after business', they probably look a lot like these:

- It's not fun anymore. Burnout is a very real issue for business owners, and an entirely legitimate reason to sell.

- You're not inclined to invest in growth. You may be comfortable with the current size and profitability of your business and aren't willing to make the capital expenditures necessary to take it to the next level.

- You're out of steam. You've built your business this far, but you don't have the resources, skills or energy to take it to the next level.

The Cost of Life on the Outside

I met a business owner who never really took much out of the business in the way of salary. The house was paid for. He and his wife went on a few vacations a year and spent a fair bit while they travelled. They ate at good restaurants every now and again. When he was ready to retire, he told me that he only needed $30,000 a year to make ends meet. But when the accountant teased out the personal 'perks' from the business accounts, (season's tickets to the hockey game, gas, auto insurance, business conferences to warm climates et al) it turned out to be more like $150,000 a year.

The lesson learned is that you need to think in terms of 'lifestyle' and what that lifestyle costs. Whatever salary or draw you take while you run your business, it won't likely be the right number for your retirement.

The other interesting quirk about business people is that income is often considered to be a bad thing. They leave as much income as possible in the business in order to avoid paying tax on it. I have actually had to counsel a business owner that 'it might be wise to pay yourself'. When you pay yourself, yes you may pay tax, but there are ways to defer it, reduce it or even split it, especially if you want to take advantage of tax-free income growth opportunities. You need to have earned income in order to build a retirement bucket. And your business needs to have a realistic picture of earnings in order to make it saleable to a potential owner.

Ready to Hand Over the Baton?

If it's not already obvious, I'll state it clearly. Even long before you're ready to hand over the baton, there's a lot of work to do to prepare the business — and yourself — for a transition. The more you prepare, the more successful the outcome is likely to be. I like to recommend at least a 5-year advance window to start working with a person who specializes in selling companies. (Just like everything else, it has become a very specialized field.)

What's Your Business Worth?

Many owners have no idea what their business is worth. On one end of the spectrum, for example, was a client who owned a promotional merchandise firm. She felt the firm was worth more than $1 million. After a lengthy search, a buyer paid her less than half that amount. Then there was a client who was about to sell his cleaning company to an employee for $200,000. After advertising the business for sale nationwide, he sold it for one dollar shy of $1 million. With the wrong valuation, you could sell your business for too little and short-change your family and your retirement. Or if you try to squeeze every last dollar out of it, you could end up missing the market and be stuck with it.

Selling a business is both art and science, and in no other area is this more evident than the valuation. While every seller wants to achieve maximum value, setting an asking price that is too high signals to buyers that you may not be serious about selling. There are firms that specialize in helping you value a business. Get help. Don't assume.

> ### Valuation: Is it Art or Science?
>
> There are a number of ways to value a business, but the most common formula is a multiple of seller's discretionary earnings (S.D.E.). It involves recasting profit-and-loss statements — adding back owner's salary, perks and nonrecurring expenses — to find the S.D.E. of the business and then using comparable data for similar businesses to arrive at an appropriate multiple.
>
> ❖

Prepare Your Business for Sale

From the experience of my clients who have sold businesses, I can offer only one general tip: there is no way to overstate the intensity with which buyers will scrutinize your business. But there are things you can do to put your best foot forward.

First, get your books in order.

Not being able to provide accurate financial statements on demand can cause a deal to unravel faster than the speed of sound.

Be ready to dig for paperwork.

During the due diligence phase, you will probably be asked to produce insurance policies, employment agreements, customer contracts, lists of patents, equipment leases and bank statements not to mention all kinds of documents you've never imagined being asked to produce.

Spruce it up.

You will also want to spruce up your business to make it attractive to buyers. Make any needed cosmetic improvements to the premises, get rid of outdated inventory and make sure that equipment is in good working order.

Never as Easy as it Looks

All sellers hope to get a full-price cash offer for their business. But in the real world this rarely happens. More often buyers will make a down payment and then pay some or all of the remainder in installments, perhaps after a period of time to ensure there are no surprises. A willingness to be creative with the terms of a transaction can go a long way toward a successful sale.

Selling a business is about setting realistic expectations, avoiding surprises and just plain hanging in there. It can be a rough journey with many unpaved roads, but the destination is well worth it.

Once you've successfully sold your business, savor an accomplishment that not every entrepreneur gets to enjoy. Whether you're trekking up Machu Picchu, retiring by the lake or starting your next venture, you did it!

Seller's Remorse

If you're asked to stick with the company after you've sold it, for a few months or a few years, think long and hard about it. As many (or most) have found out, it's not nearly as much fun as being the top dog. Most entrepreneurs are not good soldiers. The transition from commander-in-chief to back-room advisor is often harder than most entrepreneurs anticipate. Either the entrepreneur has trouble giving up control, has trouble with the idea of a collective voice, or simply finds the new owner's culture radically different from what they were used to. Sometimes, they simply cannot bear to see what the new owners are doing to their creations.

Most wrestle with the fact that they still have the responsibility, but not the authority. Can you work for a boss? Are you ready to be overruled by your boss? Can you stand the idea of getting vacation 'authorized' by the boss? Your hours scrutinized? Can your clients adjust to your new role? Can you stand to watch if the new owners drive the business into the ground?

It can be gut-wrenching even in the best of circumstances, but at the end of the day, you've got to be able to let go.

Notes for the Family Enterprise

Despite the fact that demographic trends are leading to an unprecedented wave of succession over the next 15 years, I found a pretty amazing statistic that the vast majority of Canadian small business owners do not have any kind of succession plan in place.

According to surveys by the Canadian Federation of Independent Business (CFIB), most business owners who even have a succession plan indicate their plan is 'informal.' In fact, many of those who have a successor in mind may not even have spoken to that person about it. That's kind of risky! What if the person you're thinking should take over your business isn't interested? Doesn't have the money? Or is so worried about their future, that they're even considering another job[6].

All Things Considered

At its most basic, a succession plan is a documented road map for your partners, family or key employees to follow in the event of your death, disability or retirement. It covers things like who gets the voting stock, who gets the management responsibilities, how and when debts should be repaid and any other elements that affect the business assets.

Here are some questions to get you started thinking about the future of the business without you in the captain's chair:

- How much control of the business do you want to maintain?

- Is there someone capable of running the business once you step down? Choosing a successor can be like navigating a minefield, especially if you have a choice of equally qualified children or employees. And with more than one

The Family Legacy

If you're counting on your kids to take over your business, you might want to have a 'Plan B' in place. A joint report issued by RBC Financial Group, the Canadian Manufacturers & Exporters Association and Queen's School of Business said that only 30 per cent of Canadian family-owned businesses pass the company on to a second generation, and only one in 10 is handed down within the family to a third generation.[1].

http://www.cbc.ca/news/background/small-business/index.html

❖

---

6 http://www.cfib-fcei.ca/english/article/309-sme-succession-update.html

child involved in the business, you have to decide which one gets to be boss and which ones merely get voting stock. The distribution of money and assets among siblings can be especially divisive. Your challenge: to divvy up business responsibilities and assets in a way that allows your business to survive — and preserves family harmony.

- Are there key employees who must be retained?

- Are there tax impacts on your estate or on your retirement plan? Is someone keeping an eye on the capital gains treatment? Preferred dividend treatment? Estate laws? Is there a charity you'd like to include as a beneficiary?

- How much money do you need to reach your financial goals? And how much can you afford to leave in the business for the future health of the business?

Do NOT Try This At Home

You probably already employ accountants, lawyers and other professional service providers that have expertise outside of your specific area of knowledge. They're able to offer advice and information on how to take that large asset — your business — and fulfill all of your individual financial goals. It's an epic juggling act of business decisions, investment planning, risk and debt management and tax planning.

I stress to all of my clients that it's important to look for someone who has experience dealing with business owners. Find out how long they have been in business. And don't just ask for references. Check them out too. At a minimum, look for respected credentials. An ability to communicate effectively is also vital. Business owners have unique needs and you want someone who 'gets it'. The sooner you look at the alternatives, the more options are available. As your time horizon narrows, so might your options.

No Place For Emotions

Successful business people have significant tax liabilities. That's just how it works in Canada. They spend many years building a business and minimizing their tax exposure. When it comes time to plan an exit strategy, it's a challenge to keep emotions out of the discussion.

For example, this one couple I met had built a $30 million business on an initial investment of about $1,000. It took a lifetime and they were passionate about it. But the tax implication of a $30 million sale was extreme. Since the business was jointly owned, they each had a $15 million capital gain. And they were each able to use their $750,000 lifetime capital gains exemption. But that still left them with over $14 million in capital gains. Taxed at 39% (in Alberta), they each had to pay $5.5 million in tax (although they would still clear $8.5 million each after tax.)

The couple was in their early 50s and in excellent health, but their emotions would not allow them to consider any type of planning around that capital gain. I recommended that they purchase a Joint-and-Last-To-Die insurance policy inside their holding company. The insurance proceeds would get paid into the holding company and be distributed as a tax-free dividend to their only child. Because the policy was going to cost them almost $600,000, they balked at the cost and decided that they would rather pay the $11 million in tax. They reacted with their stomach and not with their head.

Stay Flexible, My Friend

One caveat to all of the succession planning talk is that no matter what plan you make today, it needs to be flexible. Your business, your family and health situations are dynamic, and your plan needs to be able to be continually updated to make sure it's as current as possible.

$traight Talk

Start to imagine a life without your business, long before it's time.

It takes years to prepare for a sale. Start early. Stay strong.

The numbers may be big, but the tax consequences are bigger.
Don't let your emotions prevent you from making rational
decisions.

Filling Your Retirement Bucket

When you're working for a living, it's usually pretty easy to figure out where the money is coming from. It's a straight-forward transaction between you and your employer that doesn't fluctuate with the markets or get different tax treatment before or after it hits your bank account.

When you're working, the goal is to fill the largest bucket of money possible by the time you are finished work. When you retire, your 'paycheque' comes from the bucket of money that you've built up throughout your working years.

That bucket has a dizzying array of permutations and combinations for longevity, regularity, rate of depletion, estate implications and tax treatment. It's safe to say that no matter how large a bucket you've filled, it would be wise to get advice on how best to structure your cash flow. To carry on with the bucket analogy: how fast a rate of pour, the filters you apply, etc.

Most Canadians will receive retirement income from a combination of four sources:

1. Government Benefits;

2. Pension Plans;

3. Registered Savings; and

4. Other Personal Assets.

Government Benefits

As part of our country's social benefits system, guaranteed retirement benefits are available to all eligible Canadians. Here's hoping that by the time you're ready to retire, these elements make up the smallest trickle of all the funds in your retirement bucket:

Canada/Quebec Pension Plan (CPP/QPP).

CPP provides a taxable benefit if you have contributed to the plan (based on your level of contributions over the years).

Old Age Security (OAS).

OAS is a basic taxable benefit paid to all eligible Canadian citizens, age 65 or older. There are plans to revise OAS in 2020. And although it's only about $500 a month, that could be your monthly food bill.

Guaranteed Income Supplement (GIS).

The GIS is an additional non-taxable benefit available to low-income OAS recipients.

Pension Plans

Beware of Defaults

Defined Contribution Plans often rely on the individual to make choices as to how, when and where the assets are invested. This is where the 'buy and hold' can often be misinterpreted as 'buy and ignore' and in these cases the default may in fact be a Money Market Fund earning barely more than the cost of living index.*

* http://www.cbc.ca/news/background/small-business/index.html

❖

Fewer than 25% of private-sector workers have access to a workplace pension plan, although the majority of public sector employees do. Most employer-sponsored plans fall into one of three categories:

Defined Benefit (DB) Plans.

These are not very common anymore. Defined Benefit plans guarantee a certain level of pension income based on a pre-established formula that includes the number of years you were employed by the company and your salary.

Defined Contribution (DC) Plans.

In a Defined Contribution Plan, your contributions and your employer's contributions to the plan are established, but not your pension income. When you do actually retire, you'll have a choice of purchasing a Life Annuity, a Locked-in Retirement Account (LIRA), a Life Income Fund (LIF) or another registered retirement vehicle, depending on the pension legislation that applies to your plan. All of these options carry provincially mandated restrictions to make sure that you actually use the money for a retirement income, instead of a spending spree.

A Personal Pension Plan.

Some business owners will have a guaranteed life withdrawal benefit plan.

RRSPs — Where the Rubber Meets the Road

There's been enough written about RRSPs to sink a ship, so I'm not going to discuss the basics of how, where, when or why. I just wanted to outline a few quick pitfalls that I've come across in my travels in addition to 'dipping in' which we've already discussed.

Shell-shocked investing.

After the roller-coaster markets in recent years, many clients are gun-shy when it comes to equities. If you lock in today's low-interest rate RRSP-GIC, your savings are exposed to an even more insidious type of risk: lost purchasing power. So if there's one place to embrace the stock market, it's in the long-term dollars dedicated to your retirement.

Paying too much tax on the outside.

If you hold growth and dividend stocks in your RRSP and keep interest-bearing investments outside of it, you're paying too much tax. Capital gains and dividends are treated much kinder by the tax man than simple interest.

Getting fancy.

Strategies such as 'holding your mortgage in your RRSP' or 'leveraged meltdowns' (where you take out an investment loan in a non-registered investment account and use the interest payment on the loan to offset the RRSP withdrawal) can trip you up with hidden costs, regulatory complexities and legal risks.

Squirreling.

Like a squirrel hiding nuts all over the forest, spreading your RRSP accounts across multiple firms may result in additional account fees and over-complicate the tracking of your investments. Plus, in order to make proper recommendations anyone advising you should have a full understanding of all your holdings, and their combined diversification, tax treatment and risk.

Missing opportunities.

Two come to mind:

- Many employers match contributions to your RSP at work. Why wouldn't you take advantage of it?

- For some couples, spousal RRSPs make sense to reduce your combined tax bite in retirement.

Not naming a beneficiary.

RRSPs have special rules when it comes to estate planning. Best to get professional advice on what to fill in on that little blank in the application form.

Other Personal Assets

There are a number of miscellaneous sources of retirement income — some of which we've already dealt with like consulting income or part time employment, or proceeds from the sale of your business. Other sources that I won't spend a lot of time on are:

- Income from a rental property;

- A portfolio of non-registered investments such as stocks, bonds or mutual funds that provide regular payouts;

But there are also sources of income that I'd like to touch on because they can be a huge boost to your retirement bucket — or a bain.

Tax Free Savings Accounts (TFSAs).

When I talk about a TFSA with my clients, I prefer to focus on the 'tax free' and not the 'savings account' side of the equation. Of course you can put any type of investment into a TFSA — cash, money markets, bonds, mutual funds — whatever! But where it really pays to use a TFSA is with mid- to long-term money because you can use it for more risky investments where any or all of the gain would be tax-free too. Its benefits for short-term money are negligible in comparison.

I usually work out a strategy for my clients to crystallize their gains as they grow and reinvest each year. So while the TFSA touts a major benefit of having access to the funds anytime, I prefer to recommend that it should be one of the last places you withdraw funds from — just slightly ahead of your RRSP. And it's also important to consider TFSAs in your estate plan because your account can be transferred to your spouse's TFSA and remain untaxed.

The TFSA Retirement Boost

If you invest $416 each month into a TFSA ($5000/ year) starting at age 18 and earn an average annual 6% return, you'll have added $1,304,927 to your retirement bucket by age 65. That $1.3 million will give you a monthly income of $6,292 for the next 40 years... and there would still be money left over when you're 105.

A side note for your teenagers. When you're 18 and going to university, many advisors recommend you start an RRSP right away. But it might be wiser to start a TFSA. Once you're in a bit higher tax rate, you can always move your TFSA over to an RSP at no charge.

Annuities.

An annuity is basically an exchange of money for a stream of income. You can get annuities that pay jointly, individually, 'term certain', or as long as you live. There are so many different flavours of annuity that I strongly urge no Canadian should sign on the dotted line without professional guidance. If you know exactly what your fixed expenses are going to be in retirement, an annuity will provide you with the basics guaranteed.

Somewhere in Canada, a salesman is, at this very moment, posting an outrageous claim about an annuity that "has some AWESOME benefits for YOU!" I know because I see those statements regularly. Often agents sell the sizzle before the steak. It's possible those claims stretch the truth. Before you get pitched an annuity, arm yourself with the following list of questions to ask the person doing the selling.

- Is this right for me?
- How does this product fit my needs and objectives?
- How much does this cost?
- What are the fees charged against the investment?
- Which fees are optional? What do they pay for?
- What are the surrender (or early withdraw) penalties?
- How do you get paid?
- Can you please walk me through my options here?
- What are the options for the underlying investments?
- What exactly is the guarantee? Is it a withdrawal stream or an actual dollar value I can withdraw?
- What if I need more than the guaranteed withdrawal amount?

- If I don't buy the annuity with the guarantee, how much higher would my account value be in 10 years?

- Can you explain to me how the company can afford to make these promises?

To be sure, there are plenty of other questions to ask. You might not want this much detail. Then again, if you are buying an annuity, you just might want this much detail, not to mention a second opinion.

Covering the Bases

Your retirement bucket of assets can come under some serious strain if you become seriously ill at some point during your retirement. There are a couple of ways you can take some of the pressure of this kind of unexpected expense in retirement.

Critical Illness Insurance covers you for more than 20 different specified problems in life, like a heart attack, stroke or cancer (although you have to live at least 30 days in order to receive the insurance proceeds).

Critical Illness Insurance is also convertible into Long-Term Care Insurance at any age past 55 or whenever you want to retire. It pays a set amount each week or month to have you under a nurse's or physician's care or in home care, whether it's in your home or in a home.

The payout can be 'for life' and the younger you buy it, the cheaper it is. It kicks in when the doctor validates that you have two of the five prescribed adult daily living activities that you can't do.

They now also have life insurance that combines Critical Illness, Disability and Life Insurance and it works on a pool system so if you use it up on critical illness then there is no life insurance left. But it is cheaper than an individual plan.

$traight Talk

Having an RRSP is a good start, but 'buy and hold' doesn't mean you can 'buy and ignore'. You'll still need to pay attention to what's happening.

TFSAs are the greatest thing to happen to Canadian tax laws in a generation. Look into it.

It's been a few decades since investing in an annuity made good financial sense. Before you're talked into one, get some advice.

One tickbox can change your life

When you retire, there's a brief moment where you will visit the HR department and be asked about how you want to set up your pension plan. The question might be posed as casually as 'one lump or two?' but the choice you make on that form can drastically change your retirement income scenario.

Depending on the terms of your pension plan, you will be offered any or all of the following choices:

- Monthly annuity from a pension plan;
- Lump-sum transfer to a Locked-in RRSP;
- Transfer to a Life Income Fund (LIF); and
- Locked-in Retirement Income Fund (LRIF).

These may all sound like Greek to you, but before you take the advice of your HR manager (often a freshly pressed MBA with nothing at stake, regardless of the decision you make), make sure you get some professional advice. Which box you tick should be carefully considered, based on:

- The impact of taxes;
- Your RRSP contribution limit and any pension adjustment reversal;
- Your anticipated tax rate during retirement;
- Your current age;
- Your health and projected life expectancy;
- Your spouse's age and life expectancy;

- Survivor benefits;

- Bridging benefits available from the plan if you are retiring early;

- Federal or provincial pension legislation; and

- Your tolerance for risk and desire for control.

Once you make your decision, it's permanent, so make sure a professional advisor helps you weigh the pros and cons of each.

Another Box to Tick

Even if you've only made one contribution to the CPP in your lifetime, you're eligible for a pension from the government. You have to be at least 60. It does not start automatically. You must apply for it (unless you're already receiving a disability benefit, which just simply converts to CPP at 65).

In 2012, the federal government changed the rules so that you can start receiving your pension without even retiring or reducing your earnings. (Although why anyone would do this defies logic since CPP is taxable.) If you start receiving your pension before your 65th birthday, your pension amount will be reduced. If you start later than 65, your pension amount will be increased. This is another one of those irreversible decisions you need to make at retirement. The latest trend by the federal government is to hang a carrot in front of you to keep you working as long as possible.

The decision when to trigger your CPP depends on:

Estimate Your CPP

You can peek at an estimate of your CPP retirement pension by creating an account at www.ServiceCanada.gc.ca. The closer you are to the date you want your pension to begin, the more accurate the estimate will be.

❖

- whether or not you still earn an income and contribute to the CPP;

- how long you have contributed;

- how much you have contributed and the amount of CPP retirement pension you can expect to receive;

- your other retirement income;

- your health; and

- your retirement plans.

On Early Retirement

Early retirement seems to be a widely held goal, perpetrated by the successful 'Freedom 55' campaign. So the question becomes: when do you start to draw an income from your RRSPs (through a RRIF)? By law, you must start to draw an income by December 31st of the year in which you turn 72 and there are minimum withdrawals that you'll have to keep in mind. But choosing to draw an income anytime before that date is optional. All RRIF withdrawals are taxable as income.

As a general rule, I advise my clients not 'to RRIF' until the last possible moment — the end of the year that they've turned 72. But of course there are exceptions. Here's an example.

If you fully retire at age 55 and never intend to re-enter the work force, the years between retirement and 60 will be your lowest income years and therefore also your lowest tax bracket. At age 60, you will start to collect CPP which increases your taxable income. At age 65, you'll qualify for OAS (Old Age Security) so your income level may increase again. You can start to RRIF at 55 and pay the least amount of tax on that income possible. As your income grows (at 60 and 65) you can deposit the excess into a TFSA so it could continue to grow tax free.

RRSPs and RRIFs are fully taxable as income upon death and are added to your final income tax return. TFSAs are not, so in that particular case, starting to RRIF early plays an important role preserving assets for estate planning.

$traight Talk

When the time comes to make the switch from a work paycheque to a retirement paycheque, there are some decisions that can't be undone. Get some good advice.

Don't start to draw RRIF income until the last possible moment.

Use TFSAs to shelter excess retirement income from taxes both now and in your estate.

The Golden Handshake

As you arrive at work today, the boss is waiting to speak to you. The dreaded day has come ad you're being laid off or terminated. Some people are lucky enough to get severance packages and holiday pay. Others find the door locked.

Retirement doesn't always come voluntarily, or when we plan for it. You would not be the first, or the last to be 'sprung' from your place of employment with little to no warning. Even if it happens when you're nowhere near ready, it's important to get great advice on what to do with your severance package. There are ways to mitigate the tax burden on large sum payouts. Also if you have a defined benefit or defined contribution pension plan I urge you to see professional help. Some of the numbers may surprise you.

Did You Get A Fair Deal?

Severance packages include some or all of the following:

- Some form of lump-sum severance payment and/or a severance payment paid out over a set period of time, based on a formula of how long you've worked there;

- An extension of group benefits, such as medical and dental plans, for a predetermined period;

- An option to convert group life insurance to a private policy;

- Financial planning and/or 'outplacement' services for a specified period of time; and

- Options for your pension plan: keep your money in the company pension plan; transfer it to a new employer's plan;

or transfer the vested portion of your pension into a Locked-in RRSP.

Deer in the Headlights?

If your severance has come as a surprise, the options are similar to those at retirement —they often have similar irreversible outcomes and definitely have very large tax implications, especially if you choose to accept the payment as an income replacement.

Roll it into an RRSP.

Canada Revenue Agency has created special RRSP contribution rules for people receiving severance packages. In addition to this year's RRSP contribution, you can roll over up to $1,500 for every year of service in your current role prior to 1989, and $2,000 for each year of service between 1989 and 1996. The government cancelled this concession in 1997, so your years of service since then don't qualify for any additional rollovers. (Vacation and sick pay don't qualify either.)

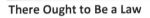

There Ought to Be a Law

Each province has legislation that establishes minimum standards for termination and severance pay. If you're unsure whether you've been treated fairly, consult a lawyer.

❖

Spread the severance over calendar years.

Your severance is taxed in the year you receive it. You can ask your employer to spread it over multiple years in order to reduce the tax impact. Of course, if you expect to be able to find new work relatively quickly, this is a moot point.

Make up your unused RRSP contributions.

If you have unused contribution room in your RRSP, you can top it up to the maximum, deferring tax until your retirement on that income. (It can also go into a spousal RRSP).

What Now?

The uncertainty created by severance is one of the nastiest by-products. What if you can't find a job right away? What if you don't want to find a job right away? What if you go back part time instead of full time? What if you need some of that severance to replace your income? These are the questions that a financial advisor can help you with to weigh the pros and cons.

In general, I advise my clients that it's in their best interest to roll as much of the severance into their RRSP and TFSA as possible for maximum tax deferral.

Are You Ready To Check Out?

So you've been pushed out the door a little earlier than you planned. Are you ready to quit the rat race and say you're retired? Should you polish up your resume, dust off your networking skills and pound the pavement? Or is it time to reinvent yourself? Go back to school? Start a business? Here's a quick checklist to decide whether it's time join the retirement party:

- Will you miss the social bonds or interactions at work? The water cooler talk? The daily banter?

- Do you need the structure that work offers? The daily routine? Can you replace that structure with new structure?

- Do you have other stuff to do?

- Do you have higher priorities, like aging parents or dependent children?

- Are you seeking a healthier work and life balance?

- Do you have other sources of income to carry you through?

Depending on your answers, you may want to consider chatting with an advisor and career counselor.

$traight Talk

If you get an unexpected severance package, don't go it alone. Get some expert advice on how to balance the tax consequences with your living expense needs.

Shelter as much of your severance from tax as possible using RRSPs and TFSAs.

The Bucket System for Retirement

Back on New Year's Eve of 2009 — after the global financial meltdown — I ran into an old friend in a coffee shop. He and his wife had retired and enjoyed regular trips to the south during the winter, so I was surprised to see him on December 31st. As the conversation progressed and their health status was revealed to be great, he confessed: "We just don't have a lot of money left and cannot afford to go".

I went home after that and was stunned. For all of us who were still working in 2008, we will all have the time to recover what might have been lost during that turmoil, but for those who were already retired, they would never have the opportunity to recover what was lost with more earnings. I realized then and there that I never want to hear one of my clients say that. So I sat down and designed what I call a 'bucket system' that would help take the fear out of retirement. Since then I've found that it provides my clients with an easy picture to calm any fears about the markets. And I want to share it with you.

Take the Fear Out of Spending

As you know, in the past two chapters we've been discussing how to fill your retirement bucket — accumulate the biggest bucket of bucks you can by saving, investing and spending wisely. And once you're retired, you will need to insert a tap to allow the money to come out — ideally in a steady stream, at just the right rate you need to consume it, so that you don't pay too much tax... and without any fear about what's happening in the bucket due to the markets and volatility.

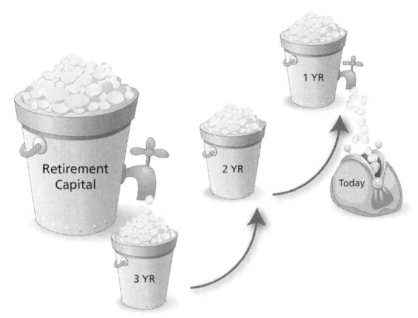

The first thing I do for my clients is to create three smaller buckets to collect income from the big bucket.

- In the first bucket, we add a year's worth of retirement income. If you need $60,000, we put $60,000 into the bucket and we invest it in a money market fund so that it will have no volatility. It won't earn much in the way of interest but it's liquid; it won't go up or down with the headlines and we can draw a regular income from it.

- In the second bucket, we invest a year's worth of retirement income into a bond fund. It might earn a slighly higher interest rate than bucket number one, and just so we can have the same purchasing power after inflation. So this gives very little fluctuation so the cash is there for continuing income needs. After that year is up, we move that money into a money market fund so it becomes bucket number one, giving us the liquidity and stability we need.

- In bucket number 3, we put a year's worth of retirement income into an 80% bond / 20% equity fund. Again, it will earn a slightly higher interest rate than bucket number one and two. We still need to keep inflation on our side. And after two years, it moves to a money market fund and becomes bucket number one, giving us the liquidity and stability we need.

Every year after that, we replace bucket number three with a new draw-down of capital from the big bucket.

No matter what, you have three years of income, guaranteed. It doesn't matter what's going on in the big bucket, because the market is rarely down for three years in a row. You won't need to read the stock markets, or check the computer to see where your portfolio is. It really doesn't matter if the level of the big bucket goes up by $20,000 today or down by $50,000 tomorrow. History has always shown that the market can go up, it can go down and it can go sideways, but generally over time, it goes up. The fluctuation does not affect you because your income is coming from one of the smaller buckets.

Managing the Big Bucket

So now that we've taken care of three years' worth of retirement income — with little to no fluctuation or market risk, now we can turn our attention to managing the big bucket.

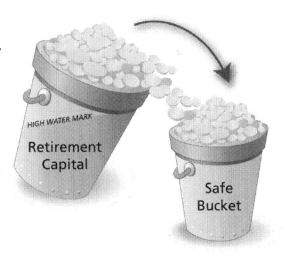

The important thing is to make sure that the big bucket is being properly cared for, planning for short, medium and long-term money, as well as 'pouring' capital into the other three buckets in the most tax efficient way.

Managing the Markets

If retirement capital is large enough to last to age 100 we put a very tight high water mark on the bucket and skim off the market 'ups' in a very systematic way, pouring the excess cash into the first year bucket. If this bucket becomes too full it might be time to purchase that new car.... Or take a fancier trip.

We invest that 'safe bucket' in secure and low-risk investments like 1-year GICs. And because the market goes up more than it goes down, we usually end up with more safe buckets than what we'd planned.

We also establish a low water mark in the big bucket. When the markets goes down — as they inevitably will — and the low water mark is reached, we simply pour money from the safe buckets back into the big bucket.

The net result is that when the markets are dropping, we're buying— just like Warren Buffet— taking advantage of low points in the market when everybody else is selling.

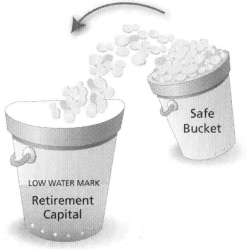

So if my distressed friend on December 31, 2008 had only had a bucket system in place, he not only would not have cashed out their equities in a fleeting moment of panic, they would have been in Texas with their snowbird friends, secure in the knowledge that they had three years of guaranteed income to ride out the uncertainty. Not only that, they would not even have noticed that the financial world had crumbled around them.

My goal for all of my clients is to provide them with a stress-free retirement. Their job is to plan their income needs for the next three years—what they want to spend it on and where. If they need a new motorhome, or want to renovate the family cottage, they just need to tell me how much it will cost, and I'll make sure the tap is adjusted to accommodate it. I'll help them stay the course by managing the water levels in their bucket and ensuring they'll always have at least a 3-year safe cushion to weather any economic storms.

On Market Volatility

"Look at market fluctuations as your friend rather than your enemy; profit from folly rather than participate in it."

~Warren Buffett

❖

Eggs in Baskets

I once met a fairly crotchety retired fellow at a networking event and he said to me with a sly wink that he had money with at least four different advisors around town. His private joke was that it was like having several mistresses who should never find out about the existence of the others. Of course I laughed politely, but in actual fact I felt a pang of angst for him. It was a classic example of the old saying: "Don't put all your eggs in one basket". I get that. Everybody gets that. But putting your eggs in different baskets is quite a different concept than hiding your baskets on different farms.

If you take $100,000 to ten different advisors, you'll likely get ten similar looking investment baskets because there's just only so much diversification than an advisor can squeeze into $100,000. But if you take $1 million to a single advisor, by its very nature, that advisor will put all of your eggs in different baskets and manage the entire farm for you. And when it comes to preserving your retirement paycheque, the idea of a 'control desk' powered by a sure-handed advisor is a critical safety factor and key to a good night's sleep.

$traight Talk

Markets go up and they go down. In a three-year cycle, you're bound to see some of everything. Use those fluctuations to your advantage.

There's nothing worse than living in fear of the morning's newspaper. When your entire future rests on the performance of your assets, make sure you get professional help.

Don't mistake the difference between having your eggs in different baskets and having your baskets at different farms.

Your Home is Your Castle

Tapping into your Home

If you've watched any Canadian television channel in the past decade, you'll have seen the advertising for reverse mortgages. The ads make it sound so simple. Even if you seriously want to or need to remain in your home — and your only hope of doing so is to tap into your home's equity in order to provide yourself with money to live on — a reverse mortgage may still simply be the worst choice you could possibly make.

You have to be over 55 to qualify, and you can receive up to 40% of the value of your home. As the name suggests, instead of you making regular payments to the bank, the mortgage now pays you. Your existing equity is the security that backs it. The only time you will ever be required to repay the reverse mortgage in full is when your home is sold, or if you move out. The advertising is quick to point out that the payments are tax free — well of course they are! It's your own money you're borrowing from your own principal residence! The ads also point out that the mortgage payments also won't impact your OAS or GIS government benefits. Again, of course not — because it's your own money, it's not income.

But here's the flip side of the coin.

If you need more than 40% of the appraised value of your home a reverse mortgage won't work. If your home is presently worth $500,000, the maximum you could get would be $200,000 but if you already owe $200,000 in a credit line or mortgage there is simply no room left to maneuver.

Another hidden feature of traditional reverse mortgages is that you have to take the amount as a lump sum and invest it in a way to generate an income. So now, not only do you have to take on an investment risk, you'll also be worrying about low-interest rates.

If you plan on selling your home within the first three years, there's a good chance that a pre-payment interest penalty will apply. It's on a sliding scale and reduces as you get closer to the third year but nonetheless it will need to be paid.

And the final kick in the teeth: if you want to pass the home on to your heirs, they'll have to pay off the reverse mortgage upon your death. This will have to be done either by the sale of the property or through remortgaging with a conventional mortgage or with cash proceeds from elsewhere.

A Better Solution

In recent years, a new product has come on the market that allows you to tap into your house equity — if you need it and when you need it. It's more like a line of credit than a reverse mortgage. You can borrow as much as 50% of the value of your house before you have to pay anything back at all. There's no minimum payment either, so if you take a few years before you start paying it back, that's okay too. The amount and frequency of the income you draw is also completely flexible. You can take a little bit each month to help boost your cash flow. You can turn the tap up or down — or off — as your spending and income needs go up or down. If you want to delay receiving RRIF payments as long as possible, this might be an interim solution that your advisor can really work with and can see you stay in your home for 20 or 30 years longer.

At some point when you finally do sell the property, yes, there might be a debt to settle. But the principle of the product is that as your house grows in value over 20 to 25 years, the portion that you borrowed may in fact be paid back by appreciation of the property. Then again, maybe not, depending on where you live and what the real estate market is like when you finally do sell.

Regardless of whether you see yourself needing the equity in your home during retirement, it's an easy process to establish this type of line of credit well in advance. That way, if you should suddenly need a new car, a new motor home, or want to lend Harvard-like tuition fees to your grandchild, you'll have the capital available to do it with a simple signature. And you can pay it back at your leisure without disrupting your retirement bucket system.

Life Lease

As I drive around the city these days, I see all kinds of retirement complexes popping up that feature a Life Lease. In its simplest sense, a life lease allows seniors to own a share of their retirement residence and accompanying common areas, which are owned and operated by a sponsoring non-profit or community-based organization.

But life leases are not simple. And they're often not fair because they're appealing to your emotions, instead of your common sense. For example, in some life leases you put up a large sum of money today to buy your share. And 20 years later, you are repaid the same sum of money, with no interest or growth. And although it sounds nice and safe, you've been robbed of purchasing power, as well as robbed of any investment growth during that time. From a strictly financial perspective, you're likely better off taking that lump sum of money and putting it towards something that will appreciate in value.

$traight Talk

Reverse mortgages are legal contracts and no matter how much they advertise, the cons almost always outweigh the pros.

If your home equity needs to form part of your retirement income plan, there are easier and more flexible ways of tapping into it than a reverse mortgage.

Life Leases are designed to appeal to your fears, not to your common sense. Before you get hooked into a life lease, get someone to crunch the numbers for you.

A Blizzard for Snowbirds

The thought of spending up to six months in a warm, sunny US sunbelt state or Mexico during Canada's cold or rainy winter season is becoming increasingly appealing and popular for millions of Canadian retirees. This trend is increasing every year, as Canada's population ages.

In the advertising, you'll see the financial planner sitting down with the client to discuss their retirement in terms of 'the most active, stimulating, satisfying and enjoyable experience of your retirement years, with life-long friendships and shared memories of good times'.

I mean sheesh! You can fly the coop in early November and return at the end of April, or you can stay with the kids until the holidays are over and leave at the beginning of the New Year. You can have the best of both worlds in terms of climate, and enjoy the benefits of both countries.

> **Try It On For Size**
>
> Despite all the positive benefits, the Snowbird lifestyle is not for everyone. (What if you don't like going back to the same place every year?) It is wise to evolve into the lifestyle in a step-by-step fashion to see if you like it, so try it for a season or two by renting a condo, house, mobile home or RV.
>
> ❖

The money picture tells a different story because when you are spending up to six months as a Snowbird, it adds a whole new layer of complexity. Family, friends, finances, fluctuations in currency exchange rates, investments, taxes, immigration, customs, housing, travel, safety and security, and medical and other types of insurance — to name a few. Of course, you can't forget about money management, financial planning, wills, estate planning, and the need for reliable professionals and other advisors.

A common language and culture, familiarity, proximity, and accessibility make the United States the destination of choice for the vast majority of Canadian Snowbirds. However, Mexico also has several locations that are popular retirement communities for Canadian and American part-time or full-time residents.

The IRS has You in its Sights

The lure of a warmer climate — and for some even the lower price of groceries and gas — seems like a well-deserved reward after years of slogging through our winter deep freeze. But rest assured that the IRS has us in their sights when it comes to getting their pound of flesh.

Depending on how long you stay (and what kind of accommodations you choose), you could trigger a tax challenge for yourself, so it's best to know the rules. (And check the rules each year before you go in case they've changed!)

If you visit the US for less than 31 days in a calendar year, you are considered to be just a visitor, and you do not need to worry about any US tax obligations.

A substantial presence

If you spend 31 days but less than 183 days in a calendar year, you may meet what is called the Substantial Presence Test. To check, add up the following:

- All the days you spent in the US during the year;

- 1/3 of the days you spent there the preceding year; and

- 1/6 of the days you spent there the year before that.

If the total is 183 days or more, you meet the substantial presence test and you are subject to US tax.

Owning US Property

Many Canadians love visiting the US so much that they snap up a second home. This was a particular

phenomenon when real estate prices fell so significantly after the recession where many Americans lost their homes due to foreclosure. So, what to do with that property when you're not there? If you said 'rent it', read on!

A 30% flat tax.

If you rent out your US vacation home while you're elsewhere in the world, the

> **A Way Out?**
>
> If your primary residential ties are with Canada you can file the IRS *Form 8840, Closer Connection Exception Statement for Aliens*. This form must be filed for each year that you meet the substantial presence test, even if no tax would have been payable on your US tax return.
>
> ❖

rental income you receive is subject to a flat 30% tax in the US before any deduction for the expenses. It's the tenant's responsibility to withhold and remit this tax to the IRS. You, as the Canadian landlord, do not have to file a US personal income tax return for that year, provided the taxes are remitted.

Rental expenses.

To benefit from the deductions for your rental property expenses, you must elect to be taxed within the US on a net basis. Before making this election, you should be aware that you must rent the property for a minimum length of 15 days per year, or the deductions will not be allowed. Even if you meet the 15-day requirement, there are other rules that further limit the amount of expenses considered deductible.

Once you've made this election, you will need to file a US return every year, regardless of whether you rent it every year. The election can only be revoked with the consent of the IRS. When you file, your rental income will be subject to the same rates as a US citizen would pay.

CRA's share.

Meanwhile, back home, you must report your US rental income on your Canadian personal tax return. You can allocate property expenses between your personal and income-generating use.

Suffice it to say that if you own a property in the US, meticulous records are a must.

A Non-Resident Tax Return

If you are a dual resident, the Canada/United States tax treaty may allow you to claim non-resident status in the US, which means you could file a non-resident return instead. As a non-resident, you are taxed only on certain US source income rather than your world income. However, you should seek advice before choosing this option because filing a non-resident return does not always result in a lower tax liability. In addition, it may affect your qualifications for a green card or residency permit.

Non-resident tax laws vary for each state; so once again, I have to say that this is not something that should be done without professional guidance.

US Taxes at Death

If you die while owning US property, your estate could also be subject to US estate taxes. Depending on the value of the US property, this could be a substantial liability for your estate. If your world-wide estate is $5 million dollars or more, and you own US property (real estate, time-shares, boats, furniture), your estate may be subject to US estate tax — even if the value of your US property is low relative to the value of your entire estate. When the IRS is tallying your US property, it's important to keep in mind that they are also counting US stocks and bonds — even if you hold them through a Canadian brokerage account.

The Trick is Not to Die Before...

In Canada we benefit from the idea of paying tax only on the financial gain on real estate. If you bought a cottage for $100,000 dollars and it was worth $200,000 dollars when you died, your estate pays tax on $100,000. In the US, you'll pay tax on the full market value. If your US property is worth $200,000, your estate is taxed at $200,000. The tax rate could be 45% or greater. Your executor could try to recoup that tax, but it could take a few years and your estate would be hung up for that long before any payouts could occur.

The trick is not to die before your US property has been disposed of in a tax efficient way.

The other important thing to keep in mind is that the IRS can change the rules. That world-wide estate figure could just as easily be dropped to $1 million, and that would mean that just about any Canadian that owns their principal residence and has a little bit of US investment can almost fall into that million dollar world-wide net worth on death.

About Timeshares

A timeshare is an ownership unit of real property entitling you to use the property for a specific period of time. Some timeshares are simply a 'right to use' the property. Others are an ownership share, which means you essentially own a piece of property. It's an important distinction and there are tax and estate planning issues to consider. If you have the 'ownership share' type of timeshare, all the same rules apply as if you owned a condominium or ski chalet.

$traight Talk

If you're thinking the snowbird's feathers fit you well, be prepared for a long list of to-do's to take care of before you go. Know the rules. The penalties are unpleasant.

When it comes to buying US property, there is nothing wrong with it if you are using it as a place to go. But if you are using it as an investment, there is probably an easier solution.

If you do decide to buy south of the border, get good advice from both a US and Canadian tax and legal perspective. And check in with both sides annually to ensure that the rules haven't changed.

'Til Death Do Us Part

As Ben Franklin so aptly said, "In the world, nothing can be said to be certain except death and taxes." Yet the subjects of money and death are difficult topics for many married couples and many families; I've met families where these two topics are even considered an absolute taboo.

It's no surprise then, that the subject of estate planning — a discussion of wills, bequests, powers of attorney, health care directives, long-term care, funeral wishes, etc — is a topic that is often avoided, even as we deal with end-of-life issues for ourselves or for a loved one.

The Four Biggest Fears

Some of the common stumbling blocks families face in planning for death are:

Fear of facing mortality.

It isn't possible to discuss an estate plan without having to acknowledge that we will die someday. That's probably why I come across so many clients who don't have wills. Oddly, talking about our own mortality can lead to positive outcomes in our financial plan, as well as improvements in family relationships.

Fear of stirring up old family conflicts.

Few families exist without conflict. Ancient hurts, buried hatchets and other potentially volatile issues can surface when decisions about money and long-term care need to be made. By avoiding issues that may stir up the conflict, the family is simply putting off the inevitable. It is far better to deal with a family conflict now than to have to deal with it at a time of crisis or despair.

Fear of creating new family conflicts.

Parents have the legal right to determine who gets what and who is to be in charge of their assets/estates. Adult children may have a completely different point of view. Many experts recommend that information — particularly if the assets are not intended to be split equally — should be shared in advance when the parents can defend their decisions, rather than withheld until after, when ill will and conflict could arise through misunderstanding.

Fear of losing control.

An older adult may fear that by making their finances an open book, someone will steal their money, or otherwise gain control over their resources (and therefore their lives). While elder abuse is a fact of life and there is (potentially) some validity to this concern, it is fortunately more of a psychological issue than a real one in most families.

As you might imagine, the discussion can go a lot smoother when there are no looming health issues, home care issues or financial crises in the wings. Since life can change unexpectedly, 'the talk' should be given a reasonably high priority on your to-do list.

Tips for 'The Talk'

So you've decided to have 'the talk' with your adult children or your parents about 'the subject that no one wants to talk about'. Given the discomfort that people have talking about money and death, it's probably wise to follow a few guidelines to ensure you get off to a good start and a fruitful (and loving) conclusion.

Choose a time where stress is minimal. For example, if Thanksgiving is a typical family flashpoint, avoid that holiday. Summer might be a great time when everyone is relaxing at the cottage after dinner. Make sure everyone knows what's on the

If Money Could Talk

agenda, and why, so that they can prepare themselves for a matter-of-fact discussion.

Meeting in person is much more appropriate than email or telephone. If long distance is a must, a video-based instant messaging system like Facetime or Skype would be better than voice only (and much, much better than text only.) Visual and audio contact is important to gauge the reaction and emotional temperature.

Remember that the individual whose estate is being planned has the right to make their own decisions. And there are lots of decisions to be made. Take your time and go slowly. Unanswered questions can be left for a follow-up meeting.

Designate a recorder for the meeting. There are many 'soft' details that need to be captured and having a written record could resolve disputes down the road.

Don't be afraid to invite expert help, such as a lawyer, accountant, financial planner, executor or mental health professional. Professionals can provide some coaching ahead of time and can give you access to information as well as strategies to make the discussions go more easily.

Once the participants get past the dreaded 'D' word, the conversation can evolve naturally. Now what? What exactly needs to be covered? Here's a starting checklist to get the discussion on track.

Will.

Where is the will located and what are the highlights of the distribution of assets and liabilities?

Executor.

Who is the executor and what financial arrangement is in place to compensate the executor?

Bequests.

You may want to leave specific assets, like a cottage or business, to certain beneficiaries while treating all of them fairly. Or, you may want to make a sizeable gift to charity upon your death. These are likely spelled out in your will, but your family should be aware of them and your reasons for the bequests. It's also an opportunity for heirs to identify specific items they'd like to be bequeathed, so that they could be included in the will. Often household items have significant meaning to one child — recipes, knick knacks, books — but mean nothing to the others. Identifying them now is a way to avoid conflict later.

Eldercare.

A large proportion of the elderly will need some sort of help in the home at some point, even if it is just while they are recuperating from an illness. While family members have historically been the first line of defense, the potential need for home care — nurse's aides, cleaners or even companions — must be considered. There are substantial differences across Canada in terms of the kinds of care available, the cost of care, residency requirements, and waiting times. Nursing homes are also a very real possibility for many families. Like help at home, these costs need to be planned for.

Tax Planning.

The tax implications on death are complex and best discussed with an advisor. Your advisor can help you minimize and defer tax and other costs arising on your death and allow for a smooth and timely transfer of assets to your beneficiaries.

Health Care Directives.

In other countries, this might be known as a 'living will' — a document to appoint someone to make decisions about your health or personal care should you become incapacitated.

Power of Attorney.

A power of attorney is a document authorizing someone to act on your behalf in a number of matters ranging from signing cheques, purchasing, selling or dealing with investments; collecting profits or commissions; managing, buying or selling real estate, — basically anything but health care. A power of attorney expires when you die; a will kicks in at death, so clearly both a will and a power of attorney are needed.

Funeral wishes.

An entire range of options exists on this subject — from prepaying and preplanning the entire funeral, to simple wishes for cremation with no ceremony. If you have specific thoughts about how you'd like to be remembered, now is the time to bring them up and share them with your loved ones.

After reading this list of topics it's easy to see where feelings could be hurt, misunderstandings could occur and tempers could flare. Your estate wishes are too important to leave to chance and best dealt with in good health and harmony.

Axes, Exes and Revenge

There's no greater ingredient for family turmoil in estate planning than the ingredient of blended families. No matter how much acrimony or strife in your family relationships, you can't cut spouses completely out of the will and give everything to children, or cut out some children to the advantage of other children. It gets tougher if you run a business and one child is helping you run that business, and the others don't. Good legal counsel — with a specialization in family law — is critical to ensure that harmony reigns after your death.

Choosing An Executor

In many family cultures, the duty of being an executor is automatically placed on a responsible adult child. Depending on family dynamics, this may not always be a wise choice since it could pit children against one another, resulting in more problems than you ever imagined possible.

The job sounds easy enough on the surface: all your son or daughter has to do is total up your estate's assets, pay any debts, and divide what remains among your beneficiaries. Unfortunately, acting as an executor can be very challenging, time-consuming and stressful. Once your executor begins the process of dealing with the estate assets, he or she is legally bound to complete the job, and can only be relieved of the duty by a court order.

Among the duties for an executor:

> **Time Out...**
>
> The Wills Variation Act allows any child or spouse of the deceased to apply to the court to vary or change the terms of the will. This Act has a six-month deadline (starting from the granting of probate). Executors must wait for six months to distribute the assets or obtain releases from each potential claimant.
>
> ❖

- Arrange a death certificate;

- Funeral arrangements;

- Payment for funeral arrangements;

- Confirm that your will is your last will with Vital Statistics;

- Cancel charge cards;

- Take care of all assets in the interim whether that means insurance, property management, taxes or whatever. Since estates can take months or even years to settle, your executor is the designated caretaker until the job is done;

- Notify your beneficiaries including any beneficiaries you've left out of your will (and who are eligible to apply to the court to change the will) ;

- Prepare and submit the probate documents;

- Contact your insurance companies and RRSP administrators with a death certificate so that money can be paid to your beneficiaries;

- Advise your local CPP office to tell them of the death and obtain any death, survivor or orphan benefits. (Note that any CPP or old age security cheques for the month after death must be returned uncashed.);

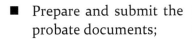

The Versatility of Insurance

Funding tax liabilities on death may become a significant task, especially if you own a business. Life insurance can provide a source of cash to pay this tax cost, and the proceeds from the policy are generally tax free.

- Advise employers and pension administrators of the death;

- File tax returns for any years for which you didn't file a return including one for the year of your death. And if your estate makes any income after your death (such as rental income or interest on bank accounts), then tax returns will have to be filed for the estate for each year after death, until the estate is wound up or paid out. The estate must pay its taxes before the assets can be distributed to the beneficiaries;

- Get tax clearance from the Canada Revenue Agency to confirm that all income taxes or fees of the estate are paid;

- Complete a full accounting of the estate's financial activities and obtain a release from each beneficiary;

- Liquidate any assets that are not being passed onto beneficiaries or in which the cash value is needing to be split among beneficiaries;

- Distribute the estate to the beneficiaries.

As you can see, if your executor also has a 'day job', make sure they know that it will take a lot of time out of their day, and perhaps for a few years. Your executors should be fully aware that they are named in your will. And if there are siblings to the executor, they need a clear understanding that your executor not only deserves to be compensated for time and effort, but that the compensation will be paid from the assets in the estate. Spell it out.

Receiving an Inheritance?

If you receive an inheritance and you put the proceeds into a joint account, it becomes shared property. As long as the income or asset stays in your name alone, it is an inheritance. If you later fund a joint asset with it (like a shared home or a joint mortgage), it then becomes shared property.

❖

It's possible that you would prefer to choose someone from outside the family to act as executor so that no individual beneficiary can 'sway' the executor beyond the terms of the will. In a sizable estate, or one with potential for disharmony, this might be the wisest course of action.

Trusts

One of the surest ways to divide assets among beneficiaries is to create a testamentary trust in your will. By creating a trust and setting out the exact participants in the trust, you can protect your beneficiaries from the subsequent marriages and divorces of any of the participants.

The assets from your estate can be directed to the trust and — because it's a legal entity — you can specify exactly how the proceeds should be allocated. For example, the principal can be left untouched and only the income distributed. Or you can create a precise distribution plan that allows some children to get a greater percentage than others. Or you can specify that children must reach the age of 25 before they can receive any of the principal, etc.

The only asterisk on this tactic is that trusts must be cashed out every 21 years and the trust has to pay the tax. Okay, there are two more asterisks:

- If any of your children live in the United States, there is an inheritance tax, so stipulating that the trust is a Canadian entity might be an important tactic to ensure that your beneficiaries do not get a big tax bill from IRS;

So Now You Tell Me

If you've been named the executor on someone else's will, my best advice is to hire a lawyer to do the paperwork and advise you of your obligations. If you do, the estate pays the lawyer's fees. Ask the lawyer how the legal fees will be calculated, whether as a percentage of the estate or on an hourly basis. But because unexpected matters often arise in estates, it may not be possible to get an exact estimate of the fees. In large or complicated estates, it's a good idea to hire a lawyer and an accountant.

Your final accounting will usually include a claim for reimbursement of expenses you've paid yourself. You'll have to decide if you also want to claim a fee for acting as executor. This fee can be up to 5% of the estate and is taxable income. If you want to claim a fee, the amount you claim should be included in the accounting that you send to the beneficiaries.

- If any of your children are married and they receive income from the trust into a joint account, the trust becomes shared property and would be divided as such on divorce.

If there is one thing I've seen over and over again in my years advising clients, it's that there is no way to predict who will join or leave your family nucleus five, ten or fifteen years into the future. Testamentary trusts may be the most important tool in estate planning to be sure that your estate is divided as you wish and that your immediate family is protected.

On Your Own

The death of your spouse can shake the very foundations of your life. In the midst of dealing with the grief and pain, there are financial matters that must be taken care of.

In addition to the routine record-keeping and bill payments, it's important to re-evaluate your insurance needs. If you have just lost your spouse and you have no dependent children, you may be carrying too much life insurance. If you are now the sole supporter of a child, you may have too little life insurance.

You may also want to take out a disability policy on yourself if you don't already have one, so that if you were unable to work you'd have money to support yourself and your family. If your spouse was the beneficiary on any of your insurance policies, you'll need to designate a new beneficiary.

Some financial decisions can usually wait for a few months, such as reviewing and making changes to your investments. Once you're ready, you'll want to create a net worth statement, a budget showing your expected income and expenses, and then assess your investment strategies.

You will also find yourself faced with lifestyle decisions such as whether to move to a smaller house or apartment, move to a different town, return to school, or travel. Having a firm grip on your financial affairs will make all of these decisions and the transition to single life a little less painful.

If Money Could Talk

$traight Talk

We're all going to die one day. It's not negotiable. What is negotiable is how we organize and manage our departure. Pick a time. Let's get the party started.

Being an executor is no picnic — not even if your estate is down to the last few cans of cat food. Don't volunteer and if you're unlucky enough to be selected, get help.

There's no way to predict who will come and go in your family nucleus after you've gone. Make sure your plans are clear, but flexible enough to ensure your intentions can be respected no matter what.

How To Screw Up Your Estate Plan With One Signature

That's all it takes. One signature can completely undo the most careful estate plan. And there are several places where a simple signature can wreak havoc on your family and the value of your estate.

Trying to Avoid Probate

Avoiding probate is usually possible when one spouse dies leaving a surviving spouse. For example, probate is not generally required if you own assets jointly with your spouse or where an asset, such as life insurance, is payable to the surviving spouse through a beneficiary designation.

Avoiding probate from one generation to the next is much more problematic and, in fact, can be more costly to the estate if changes to ownership or to beneficiary designations are done without considering tax and other implications.

Joint Ownership

If I had a dollar for every time I have come across the idea of putting the title to the parent's house in joint ownership with the children, I'd be a very wealthy man. Sad, but wealthy. The strategy that is supposed to be behind this tactic is to allow the house to transfer to the family without forming part of the estate of the parent. And while that is the initial success, the problems arise much later down the pipe quite simply because the house then becomes a taxable capital asset for the child because it is not a principle residence. When your child then turns around and is ready to sell the property, he or she is taxed on the capital gain — a much more costly proposition than anyone anticipated.

It gets worse. An even deadlier idea is putting the house into joint ownership with all your children — effectively forcing not only a capital gains challenge for all the children, but also a challenge to ensure that all of the children (and their spouses) will agree on when, where and how to dispose of the property. Add adult grandchildren, vindictive ex-spouses and unequal life circumstances (what if one of the children wants to live in the house?) and presto! Instant disharmony.

It would make far more sense to sell the property while Mom or Dad is still alive. Since it is a principle residence, the capital gain rule does not apply and the full cash value of the asset becomes part of the estate. Or if Mom or Dad is still actively living in the house, the will should dictate that it should form part of the estate and be liquidated upon death.

One final note on this strategy is that if there is an *only adult child* and that only adult child actually lives in the house as a principle residence, it's no problem at all to transfer the asset through joint property ownership. There is no tax issue and no squabble about what to do with the house in the future.

The same situation occurs when families try to decide what to do with a cottage property. When Mom and Dad are no longer able to enjoy the cottage property, there is often a tendency to want to pass it on to the next generation by putting the ownership in joint names. Once again, the capital gains rule applies. And once Mom and Dad are over age 80, they can no longer buy life insurance to cover the tax liability.

Beneficiary Designations

If you have an estate that you wish to distribute in a specific way (leaving more to one child as a reward for a sacrifice, or to compensate for a disability for example), your advisor can help you to ensure that through life insurance, trusts and specific bequests this can all be achieved. But if you make changes later (like applying for a new life insurance policy or moving RRSPs to another institution), you could completely invalidate your estate plan by naming a beneficiary which contradicts your estate plan. With one signature on that beneficiary designation form, you can completely undo all of your careful estate planning.

$traight Talk

Transferring title to a house into joint names is a tax problem waiting to happen. Unless you're an only child and planning to make it your principal residence, get tax advice first.

If you have more than one child, tread carefully in distributing your assets. They may not see things with equal clarity after you've gone.

Have your will and estate plan reviewed regularly. Even though life feels like nothing has changed, when you start to talk about it, you'll discover things have changed in a meaningful way for the tax man.

If Money Could Talk

'Til Divorce Do Us Part

There is no shortage of jokes about the high cost of divorce and I speak from first-hand experience when I tell you they're all true. Knowing your rights as well as your obligations and how to protect yourself can make it less expensive, although it's doubtful to be made any less painful.

If your marriage is in trouble, you will not feel in control emotionally. You will be overwhelmed and likely stressed out and you may need counseling to determine if divorce is the best decision for you and your family. Take baby steps, one hour at a time; there is light at the end of the tunnel, I assure you.

If you've explored all the options and you really think divorce is something you must do, here's a quick list of questions to consider before you even mention the topic to your spouse.

Your home.

Who will live in your home? Where will you live? Should you sell your home and purchase (rent) separate residences? Will you qualify for a mortgage? You must crunch the numbers to determine if the home you may be attached to (or that you don't want to uproot your children from) can be managed financially. Although some people can view a house as simply an address, many others create huge turmoil over an emotional attachment to a house. Remember, a house is not a home. It's the people that make the home.

Your spouse and children.

If you have a non-working spouse (or if you're the non-working spouse) will he or she (or you) have to return to the workforce? Be able to return to the workforce? Spousal support and child support are very big considerations. Maintaining a lifestyle, while supporting two residences is a very big deterrent to divorce.

Although not seeing your spouse every day might be a welcome relief, it's also highly likely that you won't see your children every day. This is a loss that is difficult to imagine until you're forced to make some kind of plans. Planning for holidays and vacations will be made much more complicated.

From a financial perspective, divorce should be relatively straightforward. Okay, that was a joke. Divorce can have a far greater impact on your future than any glitches in the stock market could ever have.

Children are Not a Weapon

If there are children involved, their well-being should be both parents' primary concern. Unfortunately, this is not always the case. Spouses paying child support sometimes feel that the custodial ex-spouse is 'squandering' the child support money, or that the child support is exorbitant. Child support is based on court-determined formulas, so griping about the amount of support will not garner much sympathy from the judge.

If child support is part of your divorce agreement, you are legally and morally obliged to pay it. Likewise, withholding of visitation rights shouldn't be used as a weapon to try to force a non-paying parent to cough up the child support payments. Don't use money as a weapon against your ex-spouse, or your children will end up as casualties.

Division of Property

The laws in Canada help determine how your assets are divided in a divorce. In general, assets acquired during the marriage by either spouse will be divided equally. Squabbles over assets generally only result in more of the assets going to the lawyers than to either of the divorcing parties.

On the other hand, I've also seen people settle for less than what they legally deserve because they're anxious to get it over with, hope to reconcile, or don't want to agitate the spouse (when children are involved). Don't willingly give up what you have a right to. And don't assume that your lawyer will protect your financial interests. In every case, it's worth seeking out a financial professional to assess the real value of your assets and take tax consequences into consideration.

In an ideal world, the division of property should be amicable as the numbers don't lie. If you and your spouse can remain cordial, mediation or arbitration can be far more cost-effective than the use of lawyers. If you can keep your head calm and recognize that it's just *stuff*, it's much simpler to part with. Watch the classic movie *The War of the Roses* to see just how off-beat divorcing couples can be. And then vow to do the opposite. Please.

Regardless of which path you choose — arbitrator, mediator, or attorney — you should do your homework. Agree on a valuation date with your spouse, list your marital assets and get appraisals where necessary — house, cottage, cars, boats, RRSPs, pensions, cash-value life insurance policies, stocks, bonds, mutual funds, stock options, art, antiques, collectibles etc. A realistic inventory of all debts is also required — mortgages, loans, credit cards, etc.

Getting Started

Once it's clear that a divorce is in the making, cancel any joint bank accounts and open individual accounts. Cancel all joint credit cards and get new ones in your own name. Close all unused credit accounts, and notify your creditors of your change in marital status.

❖

In some cases, I've seen divorcing couples squabble over frequent flier miles, pets, tax refunds, unpaid vacation pay, wedding presents — you name it! Decide what's important to you and let the rest go. If there's disagreement about one or more items, there are a number of fair methods of deciding who gets what. One of the most common is bartering, where one spouse takes certain items in exchange for others. Other assets can be sold so that you can split the cash; it's much easier to share cash.

You'll also need an accurate inventory of each other's income sources, which might be trickier than it sounds because accumulating vacation pay, benefits, bonuses and stock options don't always show up on the pay stubs.

The courts will likely also want to see a few years' worth of tax returns. If one of the spouses is a business owner, the tax return is not always a solid reflection of earnings, but might be evidence of the ability to 'hide' income with offsetting expenses.

Division of Debts

Often even more difficult than dividing the property in a divorce is deciding who will be responsible for the debt the couple has incurred. In order to do this, you'll need to know how much you owe. Even if you trust your spouse 100%, do yourself a favor and order your joint credit report. People have been known to run up debt without their spouse's knowledge, especially when they're contemplating leaving the marriage. Overlooking this step could cost you years in debt repayments.

Next, you'll need to agree on which debt is shared and which is in your name only (or your spouse's name only). At this point it's important to stop the joint debt from growing any larger.

There are several ways to decide what to do about debts:

- If possible, pay off the debts now. If you have savings or assets you can sell, this is the cleanest method. You don't have to worry that your spouse will leave you responsible for his/her portion of the debt, and you can start your new life debt-free;

- Agree to take responsibility for the debts in exchange for receiving more assets from the division of your property.

- Agree to let your spouse take responsibility for the debts in exchange for receiving more assets from the division of property;

- Agree to share responsibility for the debts equally. This leaves you the most vulnerable, because your spouse could stick you with the total debt. Legally, you are responsible if your ex-spouse doesn't pay up, even if s/he signs an agreement taking responsibility for the debt.

Tax Issues in Divorce

With all of the pressing issues of divorce, many people forget to consider the tax implications, an oversight that can cost you thousands of dollars and more. Tax issues include:

- Who will get the tax exemption for dependents?

- Which attorney fees are tax deductible?

- How can you be sure maintenance payments will be tax deductible?

- How can you avoid the mistake of having child support be non-deductible?

Retirement Plan Issues in Divorce

It should go without saying, but registered assets need to be treated completely separate from non-registered assets because they also contain a tax liability. Make sure that your division of assets ensures that the registered assets are shared equally, as well as the non-registered assets.

A Word About Dishonest Spouses

Harkening back to *The War of the Roses*, divorce can bring out the worst in some people, and you need to be aware that even the most honest of people may try to cheat when it comes to settling up financially in a divorce, by under-reporting income, asking an employer to delay a large bonus or salary increase, etc. Most vulnerable are those whose spouse owns a closely-held business.

Questionable transactions and other sleights of hand

- Unreasonable owner salary (too low) levels;
- Automobile write-offs;
- Personal expenses written off as business expenses;
- Petty cash abuses;
- Inventory abuses;
- Large one-time purchases written off;
- Things that temporarily drive a business into decline;
- Self-dealing and inter-family dealings;
- Sudden increases in cost of supplies;
- Sudden appearance of new suppliers or new customers;
- Sudden decrease in gross income;
- New or hidden bank accounts;
- Delaying income until after the divorce;
- Fraudulent bad debt write-offs;
- Unreported cash transactions.

Picking Up the Pieces

Given the emotions involved in divorce, many people often live in the moment, with a goal of simply getting by day by day. If you have trouble focusing on the future, you're not alone.

When your divorce is final and assets have been legally divided, change names on house deeds, stocks and bonds, and car titles, as necessary. Change beneficiaries on investments, retirement plans, life insurance policies, and savings accounts. Update your will. Check your credit report to make sure your spouse hasn't incurred debts in your name since your divorce or separation. Both parents need to re-evaluate whether they have adequate protection—disability as well as life insurance.

A financial advisor can help you to see what is possible for life after divorce and what you can do to improve the situation. Basically, most people have two choices when it comes to rebuilding their finances: increase income or decrease expenses. If you can do both, you will definitely be better off. If you need an objective eye, an advisor can help you evaluate cash flow and expenses. If you've received a lump-sum settlement, an advisor can show you how the money can be invested to provide current income and long-term financial security.

It Takes Time

People often overlook the need to plan for when support payments end. If you don't have a plan for how you'll replace the support payment income, it can leave a big hole in your cash flow and impact your ability to get ahead. By developing a post-divorce financial plan, an advisor can show you what's needed to meet future obligations, such as post-secondary education for children, and plan for retirement. There are a number of strategies to rebuild for the future including downsizing housing, working longer and spending less in retirement. It will take time to rebuild, so it's important to get started as soon as possible.

$traight Talk

Take baby steps. There's light at the end of the tunnel. I've been there. Trust me.

Children are not a weapon. If you feel like using them as such, get counseling.

Decide what's important to you and let the rest go. It makes the destination much clearer. Otherwise the only ones who benefit are the lawyers.

Dependent Adults

This chapter is certainly not for everyone and if you don't require this information, consider yourselves among the blessed. I have a disabled sister and she has been in a home for most of her life so this is a topic that is near and dear to my heart.

Whether your child has a visible disability, like Cerebral Palsy or Down Syndrome, or an 'invisible' disability like Autism or Asperger's, chances are you're constantly learning about your child's disability and trying to make the best decisions about how to deal with it — not just in the present, but also in the future. It's a fine balance between planning your retirement and planning for your child's care. You're not alone if you feel bit overwhelmed by everything, at least occasionally.

You probably feel like you have enough to do without having to navigate your way through endless amounts of information just to find out what help is available — grants, tax credits, wheelchair funding, special education funding, autism funding, respite funding, assistive technology funding — let alone trying to access it. It's offered by government, non-profit agencies and charities, so just doing your research can practically be a full time job.

Disability Tax Credit

It generally takes months to apply and receive this credit, so be sure to leave yourself lots of time to apply and also to renew every 6 years or so (they'll send you a notice to renew).

❖

Typically, provincial governments treat disability payments as a type of welfare, meaning that recipients can only receive money if they prove they're destitute. In the case of people with disabilities, recipients often qualify for benefits and special funding for equipment, but only if certain conditions are met.

The hope is that provincial disability payments and benefits would not be clawed back by amounts that are received from the disability savings plan — otherwise what would be the point? Losing the ability to have a motorized wheelchair, for instance, could mean the difference between being mobile and being stuck at home or in an institution.

Luckily, provincial governments are slowly coming on board, and a number of provinces have already decreed that the RDSP payments won't result in a claw-back of other payments.

Tax Planning

Some provinces have stand-alone disability support programs, while others recognize disability as a special qualification within the overall social support system. Generally though, for participation or qualification, the disability must be certified by a licensed physician using provincially prescribed criteria and forms. And entitlement is reduced or eliminated where earnings or assets exceed regulated thresholds.

Tax relief generally falls into these major categories:

- Deductions that reduce the taxable income;

- Disability supports deduction;

- Medical expenses;

- Attendant care expenses;

- Non-refundable tax credits that directly reduce the tax payable (but can't take it below zero);

- 'Disability amount' for qualifying out-of-pocket expenses incurred to work, go to school or conduct grant supported research;

- Caregiver amount for individuals providing home care to an immediate family member;

- Disabled children are also eligible for the Child Fitness Tax credit, which actually doubles the benefit;

- Refundable tax credits: These may result in an amount payable to the individual even where tax liability has been reduced to zero;

Unclaimed Credits?

If you discover that you have unclaimed disability-related tax credits, your advisor can help you to back-file for up to three years as allowed by the CRA, plus another potential seven years under the Fairness Package, legislation that allows the CRA to use discretion under certain circumstances.

❖

- GST/HST relief: Many goods and services used by persons with disabilities are not subject to GST / HST. These include: most healthcare services; personal care and supervision programs while a primary caregiver is working; prepared meal delivery programs; and public sector recreational programs designed for those with disabilities;

Estate Planning

Estate planning for dependent adult children is complex and there are gaps between federal and provincial systems.

If you have more than one child, the issue of whether to treat all of your children equally or equitably needs to be decided first because the tax systems deal with special needs children differently from other children. Important credits may be available to supporting parents. Most importantly, the balance of the RRSPs or

RRIFs, which are usually fully taxed on the death of the last parent, may in some cases be transferred to the special needs child without tax. These funds may be structured in a Lifetime Benefit Trust in the case of mental infirmity, for the exclusive benefit of the child during his or her lifetime.

A certificate from a physician or other qualified professional might be required in order to access some benefits, so before counting on this benefit, it's best to check the details thoroughly with an expert in special needs estate planning.

Beware of the Inheritance Trap

The short story is that an inheritance greater than $100,000 will directly impact your child's benefits. If you have sufficient assets to completely discount any government support, that's ok, but many people fall into a trap unknowingly.

If the inheritance is less than $100,000, your child can receive $5,000 a year from a trust fund (that you set up from the inheritance) on top of disability expenses.

Money that is left in reserve in a discretionary trust will not reduce the pension until applied to the benefit of your child.

It's challenging enough to predict what income taxes will

Tax Rollovers on Death

Parents or grandparents of a financially dependent person with a disability can roll over their RRSP or RRIF to an RDSP upon death, provided there is adequate contribution room available. Unfortunately, these roll over provisions do not trigger grants from the Federal Government.

❖

be payable on the settlement of your estate, without knowing what impact it will have on your adult dependent child's inheritance or trust benefit. In addition to exploring the RDSP, you might also want to consider purchasing life insurance.

A Quick 5-Pack on the RDSP

If you or a family member qualifies for the Disability Tax Credit, then you should probably also be taking advantage of the RDSP — the Registered Disability Savings Plan.

This plan was designed to offer a way to provide long-term private funding to people with disabilities. It was initially conceived by Canadian parents of special needs children who wanted to be able to put money aside for their children's adult years, in addition to an education savings account.

1. In order to qualify for the RDSP, a person with a disability must first qualify for the Disability Tax Credit. They don't need to actually be taking advantage of the Disability Tax Credit; they just need to qualify for it.

2. A Registered Disability Savings Plan (RDSP) can be set up by the person with a disability or their parent or guardian. Contributions of up to $200,000 can be made now, for use in the future.

3. Once your child reaches age 50, the grants stop. You can contribute to the RDSP until your child is 60. Income must start to be taken from the account by age 60.

4. The principal amount is not tax deductible from your income but the gains and government grants are taxed in the hands of the beneficiary when withdrawn.

5. Depending on family income, if you make a contribution of $1,500 per year, the federal government will add a grant up to a maximum of $3,500 per year. The maximum lifetime grant is $70,000 or when the beneficiary of the plan reaches age 49, whichever is sooner.

Your Executor Holds the Key

In creating your will, you will need to name an executor to administer your affairs upon your death. You are entrusting this person with the obligation to ensure that your estate plan unfolds as it was intended — and nowhere is this more important than with the future of your adult dependent child in the balance. This might be the best example of all when a professional executor or trust company is the most appropriate choice, rather than a family member or sibling.

A good estate plan gives the trustee permission to adjust your plan to accommodate circumstances as they arise.

No estate plan, no matter how comprehensive, can ever include all variables that might occur over time, both before and after your death. Therefore, the most important aspect of your plan is that it should be flexible. The value and nature of your assets might fluctuate. Your special needs child might or might not qualify for special tax status at the time of your death. Government assistance to challenged beneficiaries might waiver. Your child's needs are not static. Your estate plan must make good sense if you die tomorrow, but it must also stand the test of time.

Committeeships

Another important consideration is who will make personal, medical, legal or financial decisions for your child after you've gone. It can be divisive to leave this responsibility to a sibling, especially if there are multiple siblings. This is where a committeeship (pronounced caw-mi-**tay**-ship) could enter the mix if you have not adequately declared how your child should be cared for.

A committeeship is a person appointed by the court to make decisions for someone who is mentally incapable, including decisions about where the person will live. Appointing a committeeship is a very serious step because it takes away a person's right to decide things for themselves. It is usually a last resort when nothing else will work. Only the court can appoint a committeeship of the person.

A family member or close friend, or a trust company, can apply to fill this role. The Public Guardian and Trustee may apply to court to be the committeeship if there are no suitable friends or family willing to act, or if there is a conflict among family members.

The Public Guardian and Trustee also reviews all applications to appoint a committeeship to ensure they are reasonable and appropriate and that the person applying is suitable. The Public Guardian and Trustee then makes recommendations to the court about the application.

Limits to the Committeeship

A committeeship has the same powers to deal with the person's estate and affairs as the person has when they are capable. But there are limits. For example, they can't make a will or estate plan for the person, or vote on behalf of the person, or have the person get married. The court might also impose some limits to the Committeeship's powers.

❖

Lifetime Benefit Trust

The Lifetime Benefit Trust is a personal trust that can be set up in your will where you can leave your RRSP or RRIF assets to the trust for the benefit of your dependent adult child (assuming he or she meets the definition of 'mentally infirm' and was financially dependent on you at the time of your death.)

Your child must be the sole beneficiary of the trust, and can receive income or capital (that is, the principal amount in the trust) at the discretion of the trustees, who you name. The trustees don't have to pay out all the income to your child, but they are required to consider his or her needs, comfort, care, and maintenance.

The trust must then purchase a Qualifying Trust Annuity with the RRSP or RRIF proceeds, and the trust will receive the annuity payments as the annuitant. The annuity must be for the life of your child or for a fixed term equal to 90 years minus his or her age. Any amounts paid out of the trust to your child will be taxable. The fair market value of the annuity at the time of your child's death will be taxable to the child upon his or her death.

Trusts

Proper trust planning is perhaps the biggest and most important part of estate planning that is intended to leave assets behind for the well-being and benefit of disabled heirs.

Unfortunately, having assets, even the proceeds from an insurance policy, will cause trouble for beneficiaries who are dependent on income-tested benefits. Trusts — known as Henson Trusts and named after a

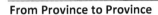

From Province to Province

One final caveat: the laws are different in every single province, so if you move from province to province, you'll need to check in again to make sure all of your wording is down pat and relevant to your unique circumstance.

precedent-setting case in 1989 — can be established, but must include very specific wording to keep from impacting government assistance payments.

For example, a trust must include a non-vesting clause that should make it clear that the trust beneficiary does not own the assets; the funds are held in trust, to be distributed at the sole discretion of named trustees. Other trusts holding assets under $100,000 can also be established under certain circumstances.

Insurance

Two types of life insurance are also often recommended to clients with adult dependent children:

- T-100 or Term Insurance to the Age of 100 is relatively affordable and the premiums are fixed; and

- Joint and Last Survivor insurance is one in which the premiums cease after the first parent's death.

The trick, however, is getting the insurance properly designated to your child's trust. The formal registration of the beneficiary is often relegated to the clerical staff at any insurance company, so it's important to make sure that it has been done correctly once the paperwork has been returned to you.

This is a superficial and over-simplified version of the detailed knowledge that's required to set up an estate properly. It's critical to choose an advisor — or multiple advisors — with directly related experience.

If the advisor you normally work with doesn't have direct experience, he or she needs to refer you to someone who does. It may cost money to do it correctly, but you will rest much easier knowing it was done right because it can't be fixed once you've passed away.

$traight Talk

If you have more than one child, the issue of whether to treat all of your children equally or equitably needs to be decided first because the tax systems deal with special needs children differently from other children.

It's a fine line between leaving a legacy for your adult child and having their benefits dashed because they no longer meet some sort of government needs test. Get advice specific to your child's disability.

By now you probably already know this, but as the primary guardian of your dependent child you need to follow a policy of 'trust but verify' in all your dealings to be sure that the proper boxes have been ticked.

The Peanut Butter Generation

Stuck in the middle with you

Looking after an aging parent is certainly not a new phenomenon in the 'circle of life', but given that women are choosing to have babies later in life, we're becoming sandwiched — between raising our children and caring for parents. And of course, as with most things, our patience and our strength to deal with the situation seems to diminish with age. It's a double-ended candle and it can burn out even the strongest of caregivers.

When you've become the peanut butter holding the whole family together, you might be tempted to invite an elderly parent to move in with you as a way to juggle their needs with the needs of your spouse and children. Here are ten essential discussions to have with your parent before mom or dad is on your doorstep:

Meals: Will your parent eat all meals with your family, or only join you on special occasions? Only when invited? If your parent isn't eating with you, how will they prepare meals? (What about grocery shopping, cooking, storage, clean-up, etc.)

Housekeeping: Will you combine chores? Or divide them up? Will your parent look after his or her own room? Help around the house as a whole? What about laundry?

Access: Will your parent use your TV, computer, kitchen or car? Will you have access to theirs?

Babysitting: Is your parent willing to babysit your children? If so, how often?

Privacy: Does your parent expect to have a private bathroom in your home? A lock on the door to their living area? Will he or she come along on family vacations?

Compatibility: Does your parent keep similar hours to your family? Does your house have to be quiet after a certain time of night? Do you all agree on smoking? Pets? Cars? Drivers?

Renovations: Do you need renovations to your home to accommodate your parent? If so, who is paying for them? Does your parent expect to have a private entrance? A kitchenette? A separate phone line? Additional TV cable packages?

Social: Does your parent expect to invite friends, bridge club members or other people to your home whenever he or she wants to? Will they be included when you socialize or have visitors?

Chauffeuring: You probably already are the head driver, but will you be called on to drive your parent to appointments or activities? Are there alternates? When can they be called upon?

Money: Will your parent share in the cost of monthly household expenses? Can your parent afford to pay for his or her share of travel? Need additional help with daily living such as nurses, meal preparers, housekeeping, etc.? If so, can your parent make these arrangements on his or her own or are you expected to help find and hire them? Can your parent afford this help?

It is never an easy choice but it can work if you have a solid understanding in place and open lines of communication.

A Few Words on the Funeral Industry

It seems if there were any chapter in this book that would logically hold a few paragraphs about the funeral industry, the chapter on aging parents wins the day.

Most of us don't plan funerals often, so when the occasion arises for us to take the lead, we're often inexperienced (or at least out of practice) and trust the expertise of the professionals. But those who do it for a living are well aware of the potent powers of love, guilt and loss on a grieving family.

A conventional funeral will usually include a number of 'miscellaneous' charges that you might be able to tackle on your own or delegate to a niece or nephew. Thank you notes, memorial cards, prayer cards, decorations, floral arrangements and other esthetic details come to mind immediately.

Still other charges—limousine rental, preparation of obituary notices, purchase of a monument, urn, marker or headstone might seem like they're the sole domain of the funeral director, but they can also be tackled on your own, avoiding the markup. You can even purchase urns and headstones on the internet.

Funeral Industry is changing

Large corporations have been buying out smaller funeral homes in recent years. They keep the same name on the door and they may keep some of the old employees around too. But make no mistake; the price list has gone up!

❖

Ask for receipts on all cash advance items such as 'grave opening', 'clergy honorarium', 'organist', etc. Make sure you ask if the funeral director will be marking up these fees. If you know the clergy or organist yourself, you may prefer to make the arrangements directly with them. (Although not many of us know any grave diggers—you may need to leave that one to the experts.)

Many costs are listed as 'givens' when they may in fact be only 'common practice'. Take embalming for example.

Embalming is not required by law.

Embalming is not required by law unless you're moving the remains to another province or territory, or out of the country. Yet, in most funeral homes, embalming is the default. So unless you specifically decline embalming, funeral homes will go ahead with the procedure and charge you for it (up to $3,000 or more).

If you want a funeral with a viewing, then embalming may be insisted on by the funeral home but it is definitely not required by law; immediate burial, cremation or a closed-casket ceremony are three ways to offset the argument and save cash.

The facts are:

- Embalming doesn't provide a public health benefit;

- Temperature has more to do with the rate of decomposition than whether a body has been embalmed;

- It has no religious roots (some religions even consider it a desecration); it's only a common practice in the US and Canada and therefore it's not the only way to show 'proper respect for the body';

Money is a Tool for the Living

Grief and bereavement can make people irrational. You may not want to think about how much it's going to cost, but keep in mind that money is a tool for the living. An economical funeral in no way cheapens the contribution of the loved one or your memories of their lifetime.

One caveat: if you refuse embalming, watch out for 'refrigeration costs'. It doesn't cost more than $20-50 per day to refrigerate a body, so don't pay too much.

Cremation.

In the pursuit of economy, many families choose cremation because you don't have to buy a casket or a cemetery plot. But just like every other funeral decision you make, cremation can also be a cash-register-ringing option if your emotions are being played.

According to the federal government's Canadian Consumer Handbook, funeral homes must enclose the body in a container that is "combustible, of rigid construction and equipped with handles". That leaves a pretty wide variety of options available and you'll see myriad choices in reasonable to extravagant price ranges.

If Money Could Talk

Keep in mind that comfort is not a requirement for the deceased. And since the container is about to be burned at high heat, choosing one that is made of anything more rigid than cardboard is a sure way to increase profitability for the funeral director.

After cremation, all that usually remains of the body is a few pounds of pulverized bone and ash. These materials represent no health risk. You're free to take the ashes in any container you see fit. Most funeral homes will store the ashes in a plastic bag within a cardboard box until you decide what to do with them. You will be pressed by the funeral director to choose an urn from their showroom, but you can also bring a container of your own choosing or again, purchase one online. There are no rules. You could even choose a container with a special meaning to the deceased: a vase, a cookie jar, a Crown Royal bag or whatever.

Casket Capers.

The price of a casket can easily add up to half the cost of a funeral. Prices range from a few hundred to several thousand dollars. Less expensive caskets are not usually on display, so you'll have to ask to see them. (You can even purchase a plywood casket if you ask.) In some areas, you can save money by renting a decorative casket for the funeral and graveside service. Discount casket stores have opened up in many cities and you can even purchase caskets online with 24-hour delivery guaranteed.

Canadian law dictates that a funeral home cannot:

- Refuse to accept a casket that you've purchased elsewhere;

- Charge you a fee for accepting the casket; or

- Increase other prices on their written price list.

Keep in mind that the service (or where the casket or urn came from) does not matter to the deceased—only to those left behind. Ask friend or relative to accompany when you decide what products and services you need in order to create a rational and respectful memorial.

$traight Talk

It's the stuff of sit-coms, but having your parents live with you takes a great deal of patience, understanding and cooperation. Discuss the rules ahead of time. You'll be glad you did.

Most of us don't make a habit of planning funerals, so take a few minutes to learn the inside tricks that are made to sound mandatory.

The funeral industry has made its fortunes on guilt and loss. Remember, money is a tool for the living. Respect is not measured by the quality of satin or the weight of coffin. It's from the heart.

Leaving a Legacy

Provinces in Canada are completely different when it comes to wills and estates, but there are four basic ways to create a will in Canada; not all of them are good ways.

1. A formal will, signed by you in the presence of witnesses (and usually prepared by a lawyer);

2. A notarial will, only used in Quebec (prepared by a notary and witnessed);

3. A holographic will — a will prepared entirely in your handwriting (never typed, nor audio or video like in the movies) and only signed by you — with no witness;

4. A store-bought or online will 'kit' where you fill in the blanks.

Simply stated, when you consider the consequences of not having a proper formal (or notarial) will, it's just not worth doing it any other way. The cost is well worth it when you consider the potential problems you'll avoid if improper wording is used or the document is not properly signed.

Witness and Beneficiary

The beneficiaries of your will cannot serve as witnesses to your signature. Nor can your spouse. Nor can the executor of your will. These rules exist quite simply to prevent a conflict of interest. Make sure your will is properly prepared, worded and executed.

❖

Holograph Wills

I've heard some people suggest that for young adults a holograph will is good enough — especially if money is tight. But even in the case of a young person, it's important to realize that a holograph will is only valid in 7 out of 10 provinces in Canada. In the United States, only 19 of 50 states recognize a holograph will and it's not recognized at all in many countries around the world. So given the rate that young people migrate and a propensity to cohabitate a holograph will may be invalid when it's needed most. Banks, government agencies, lawyers and the courts are rightfully wary of hand-written wills. The cost of interpreting a hand-written will by a lawyer and a court is more expensive than paying for a properly drafted will in the first place.

My short summary: a holographic will should only ever be recommended to somebody who is pinned beneath a boulder and about to draw their last breath.

Drugstore Wills

Another bad idea is preparing your will with one of the many pre-printed forms or computer programs currently available. They are inexpensive, but your savings are small compared to the legal costs your beneficiaries might have to pay to settle your affairs. The courts are extremely picky about wording and if your will is not worded properly, it could be legally invalid. And if it's not clearly worded, it will lead to even more problems. For example, "divide my estate

Finding help

Any lawyer can draft your Will for you – right after handling your divorce, helping you buy your house, setting up your corporation, reviewing your taxes, and helping you with your car accident. These lawyers are generalists, not specialists. If your estate is complex, please seek out a specialist.

❖

equally between my sisters and my friend Brandon" can have at least five different interpretations. And since you won't be around to clear up the confusion, it's a recipe for disaster.

The kind of thing that these DIY kits are notoriously bad for is considering the what-if scenarios. What if your beneficiaries are not able to receive the bequest? What if your beneficiaries are run over by the same bus as you? What if your executor is in jail or has had a stroke and is unable to perform the duties? What if there are children or spouses or jointly held property?

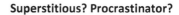

Superstitious? Procrastinator?

We all like to think we will live a long time, and there's always plenty of time to address this topic 'tomorrow' or 'when the kids are grown' etc. Reality has its own plan for you. Accidents and sudden, fatal illness happen. Why tempt fate by going through life unprepared?

❖

All your potential what-if scenarios need to be covered and all Executor and Trust powers need to be included.

Who Cares. I'll be Dead.

The last thing you want to do is to die without a will. The courts will consider that you have died 'intestate'. Right off the top of the list, your children would become wards of the province with no say as to where and with whom they will live. Similarly, if your will can't be found, or is deemed to be invalid (see above), the courts also consider you to have died intestate. Each province has laws to deal with this situation, but basically the laws dictate that the debts (including taxes) are to be paid first and anything remaining can be divided among your heirs. The main difference is that you cannot control what the courts decide. The standard order of priority is:

spouse, children, parents, brothers and sisters, and more distant family such as nieces and nephews.

Perhaps more important than the order of priority that the courts choose is the hassle it leaves behind for your family. A family member will need to apply to the courts to act as your estate administrator. Once the court provides a 'certificate of appointment', the administrator must identify and settle all debts in your estate, including tax returns. If anything remains, the administrator has to figure out how to divide the rest of the estate and must try to find your legal heirs (not always as easy as it sounds) and get their agreement about how the assets should be divided. And if there's one thing that goes smoothly — tongue in cheek here — it's getting people to agree on what's fair when money is involved.

When a Dollar is Not a Dollar

Naming a beneficiary of an RRSP or RRIF (other than a spouse or child) is never a good idea. Although the beneficiary receives the entire RRSP or RRIF, your estate will pay the income tax owing on the RRSP or RRIF at death which may be nearly 50% of its value.

❖

And, now, to play out the worst case scenario, what if no one in your family is willing (or able) to act as your administrator? In that case, the court may appoint a trust company to undertake the task and the trust company will charge a percentage of the value of the estate for their services. The cost far outweighs the initial expense of having a properly drafted will in the first place.

And Furthermore

One of the characteristics of a great estate plan is that it is broad enough and general enough to stand the test of time. I've often come across self-drafted wills that are founded on the notion that they will give away their estates in pieces — the house to their son, the cottage to their daughter, a bank account to a cousin, the car to a friend — you get the idea. There are exceptions, of course, but generally it is not a good idea to mention particular assets in your will.

Firstly, your assets are constantly changing. As a result, you may not have the same assets at your death that you had on the day you signed your will. Second, all assets do not have the same tax consequences at death. Without considering the tax consequences for each asset, one beneficiary may get much more or much less than you intended.

Specifying that an asset is to be left to a particular beneficiary is only advisable in certain circumstances. For example, you may decide to gift your stock portfolio to a charity so that your estate receives the very favourable tax benefits for doing so and, of course, you want to benefit the charity. Or you may want a particular family heirloom to go to a certain cousin so that it stays in the family.

Your Will

If you've created specific instructions in your will about how your accounts should be distributed, you can name your Estate as your beneficiary on RRSPs, RRIFs and Life Insurance policies so that no misinterpretation can occur.

❖

Life Insurance After Age 50?

In its purest sense, the intention of life insurance is to provide an income replacement for your family after you die. But once you've passed the age of 50 and assuming your children are fully functioning adults, why would you need life insurance?

Of course, things do not always work out the way the story books tell us they will when we are younger. Job losses, divorce and other financial setbacks mean that savings do not accumulate the way we hoped they would. If you had kids later in life, they might still need support when you're 60. Beyond that, with financial troubles, many older kids are returning to the nest — like a revolving door — and sometimes with their own kids in tow! It's easy to see how that mortgage that should have been paid off in 15 or 30 years may still be outstanding because of a refinance or move.

Of course, you may have had life insurance coverage before. Your term life insurance policy might have expired, or you had some group coverage at a job where you no longer work.

After age 50, and even well into retirement years, you can still find a policy. Of course, the choices will depend upon your health, budget, and some other factors.

In general, a fairly healthy 70-year-old should still be able to find a 10-year term policy, but could not expect to find a 30-year term. At this life stage, permanent life policies may be better choices. Of course, you may have to accept a lower face amount to keep the premium rates affordable.

But just because we have reached middle age, or even retirement age, does not mean we have outlived their need for life insurance.

Final Expense Policies.

This is the type of coverage that is common associated with seniors who are already retired. It is actually a whole life policy that has been designed for an easier application process so people from about 50 to about 70 (sometimes 80) years of age can be issued a policy. They usually have a fairly small face value ($2,500 to $25,000) and are usually intended to pay for funeral costs and maybe settle a few debts. These are the policies you see advertised on television where they tout the fact that only a few health questions will be asked beyond 'screening for terminal illnesses' for example. Death benefits should be immediate too, so this means that as soon as the policy is issued, the insured person is covered for the full value of the death benefit.

Guaranteed Issue.

Another final expense policy asks 'no health questions at all', and it is always issued. How can insurers do this? Well, these policies are usually a bit more expensive than the 'only a few questions' policies. But the main difference is they do not have an immediate death benefit. In other words, you have to live long

110   If Money Could Talk

enough to pass the elimination period, which may be 2 or 3 years, before the full death benefit will paid. This is how insurers can offer to cover everybody.

Most of the time, guaranteed issue policies will refund premiums, or sometimes pay a partial benefit, if you die before the time period is up. Having to wait for the full benefit is a drawback, but since premiums are refunded, this may be a good option for some applicants. In fact, it may be the only option for some.

Business Insurance.

Another common reason why older people need life insurance is for their business, in order to transfer an estate or guarantee financing. The use of insurance in small and medium-sized businesses is complex. If you own a business, there are all kinds of risks you can cover off with life insurance.

Other Reasons.

These days, many people are redefining the traditional retirement age. In my experience, almost anybody can find an insurer who will write a policy they need, if that person is willing to pay the premiums.

Mortgage Insurance

Picture this: you've just spent months shopping for your dream home and you're finally signing the mortgage paperwork. Your banker casually asks you whether you'd like to have mortgage insurance (it's as casual as asking if you'd like fries with that). It seems like a good idea — protecting your family against unforeseen death of one of the mortgage payers. And it's so simple — they will conveniently just tack the premium onto your monthly payment.

The basic premise of mortgage insurance is sound but the problem is that in many cases it's a blind rip-off. It's another example where one mark in a check box can make a mockery of your financial plan because this type of coverage is significantly more expensive than a traditional insurance policy.

Although it's not as earth shattering an impact as choosing the wrong tick box for your pension, it is one of life's annoyances that get a financial planner's dander up for three main reasons:

- As your mortgage balance goes down, the mortgage insurance face amount also goes down, but your premiums stay the same. On the other hand, if you have a separate policy, your face amount stays the same, your payments stay the same, even as your mortgage shrinks.

- Mortgage insurance through a lender is not portable so if you switch banks, pay off your mortgage or move to a new home, the insurance lapses. An individual insurance policy through an insurance company is owned by you — you can keep no matter what happens to your mortgage.

- Mortgage insurance through a lender only pays out a benefit equal to the mortgage, even if both spouses die. Individual policies will pay out twice the amount in the event of a simultaneous death.

If you think you'd be receiving all these benefits when paying the premium from your mortgage lender, think again. A 51-year-old male will pay $0.64 per thousand dollars of mortgage amount on a mortgage life insurance plan with BMO[7]. On a $500,000 mortgage, this translates to $275 per month. That same male can apply for a 20-year term insurance policy of $500,000 for roughly $174 a month. That's a savings of over $1,200 per year. And over the course of the mortgage, $24,000 — not bad for a few minutes of research.

The moral of this story: a lender's mortgage insurance offers convenience. But this convenience comes at a price — inflexible coverage, and in most instances, significantly higher premiums.

---

[7] http://www.bmo.com/home/personal/banking/insurance/mortgage/life-insurance

Accidental-Death Insurance

Major catastrophes such as car wrecks and fires are covered under other policies, and so is any harm that comes to you while at work. Accidental-death policies are often fraught with stipulations that make them difficult to collect on, so skip the hassles and get life insurance instead.

6 Ways to Leave a Legacy

Charitable donations are a nearly invisible but deeply important activity in Canada. They are the glue that holds our social fabric together. And Canadians are a generous lot. Almost 5.5 million Canadians made a financial donation to a charitable or non-profit organization during 2015. Those donations totaled $9.1 billion. [8]

There are over 86,200 registered charities in Canada that are eligible to receive charitable funds[9]. These organizations, both large and small, are committed to making a positive change in the world and rely heavily on the support of donors to continue their good work.

Planned giving — leaving a legacy to a charitable organization — is encouraged by the federal government with specific tax benefits, so here are the five most popular ways that not only do good for the charity, but can also provide tax benefits to your estate.

Gift through a will.

You can specify a cash bequest through your will to a registered charity. You can also specify a percentage of your estate. The benefit of making a donation this way is that your estate is entitled to a tax credit for the final income tax return and you can reduce your estate tax liability.

---

[8] http://www.cra-arc.gc.ca/chrts-gvng/lstngs/menu-eng.html as of 2/28/2017

[9] http://www.cra-arc.gc.ca/ebci/haip/srch/basicsearchresult-eng.action?s=+&k=&p=1&b=true

Gift of stocks, bonds or mutual funds.

If you own publicly traded securities, you could owe taxes when you sell them (if they're not in your RRSP or RRIF). However, you can donate the shares, mutual fund units or bonds to charity by what is known as an in-kind transfer. The charity can then sell your securities and issue a receipt for the fair market value. Neither you nor the charity are taxed on any capital gains.

Gift of RRSPs, RRIFs.

You can simply designate the charity as the beneficiary of your RRSP or RRIF. The assets don't pass through your estate and your estate will receive the tax receipt in the year of death.

Gift of life insurance.

Similarly, if your life insurance policy no longer fits into your financial plan you may want to consider donating the policy to charity.

Charitable Remainder Trust.

With a Charitable Remainder Trust, you place certain assets in a trust (like real estate, cash or securities) and receive a net income from those assets for life. You also receive a tax credit in the year the gift is made. The charity receives whatever remains in the trust after your death.

Set up your own foundation.

You don't need to be a multimillionaire to start a foundation of your own. In fact, the majority of private Canadian foundations have assets of less than $1 million. There is no minimum requirement for capital endowments but you probably need to invest enough capital to be able to distribute at least 3.5% of invested assets without encroaching on the capital.

Of course, it's not as easy as it sounds. There will be costs associated with incorporating, registering and organizing the foundation. Depending on the size of it, there may also be costs associated with office space and administration. You should estimate a minimum of $5,000 up to a maximum $25,000 (for more complex foundations) in fees and costs associated with start up, and also think about the operational costs on a yearly basis, which could be lower if you have a way of sharing expenses and using volunteer staff.

Do Your Homework

If you're interested in establishing a lasting gift to charity, there are several steps to take to ensure your gift will be treated as intended — both by the Charity and the CRA. A quick check-up with an advisor can help you get started on the right path to make it happen.

$traight Talk

A holographic will should only ever be recommended to somebody who is pinned beneath a boulder and about to draw their last breath. Drug store wills are about of the same value.

When we were young, life insurance was all about protecting the lifestyle of our families if we passed prematurely. After age 50, life insurance is all about protecting an estate from taxes. Look into it.

If you're interested in establishing a lasting gift to charity, there are several steps to take to ensure your gift will be treated as intended — both by the Charity and the CRA.

Protect Your Earning Power

Most people will earn 2 to 3 million dollars in their lifetime. And if you get hurt at age 50 or 55 (your best earning years) and had to take a year or two away from work, it would not fit well with your future plans at all. And what if, after your recovery, you couldn't do what you are trained to do and you have to take a lesser-paying job to make ends meet?

Disability insurance can provide you with financial security by replacing a portion of your earnings when an accident or illness causes you to become disabled and unable to work or earn an income.

Accidents and illnesses are a fact of life. They could happen to anyone at any time. Here are two scary stats I found:

- 1 in 3 people, on average, will be disabled for 90 days or longer at least once before age 65;[10]

- The average length of a disability that lasts over 90 days is 2.9 years.

Many people have a disability insurance policy through their workplace. But if you're a professional or a business owner, you'll have to buy this type of insurance separately. You can purchase a policy that ensures that you can come back to the same occupation, and if you can't do your same occupation, the policy will pay you until you are 65. Many disability policies come with a 'return of

---

[10] http://www.canadalife.com/003/home/products/disabilityinsurance/index.htm

premium', which ensures that you'll get at least 40% of your premiums repaid.

The Big Three

Cancer, heart attack and stroke are the three most common critical illnesses, occurring across all ages in Canada.

- According to the Canadian Cancer Society, approximately 202,400 Canadians are diagnosed with cancer each year[11], and thanks to improved medical treatments, most of them will survive.

- According to the Heart and Stroke Foundation of Canada[12] 50,000 Canadians are diagnosed each year with heart failure:

- There are over 62,000 strokes in Canada each year. That's one stroke every nine minutes. In fact, about 405,000 Canadians are living with the effects of stroke[13];

  - After age 55, the risk of stroke increases sharply;

  - 10% of stroke patients are diagnosed as having prior dementia and an additional 10% develop dementia after their first stroke; more than a third of patients develop dementia after a second stroke

  - The number of people with vascular dementia doubles every five years after age 65

Yet, while medical treatments and survival rates have improved, most health plans haven't kept pace with the changing needs of patients. Provincial health plans can't help with personal finances. As highly regarded as our Canadian health care system is, it cannot

---

[11] http://www.cancer.ca/en/cancer-information/cancer-101/cancer-statistics-at-a-glance/?region=bc

[12] http://www.heartandstroke.ca/-/media/pdf-files/canada/2017-heart-month/heartandstroke-reportonhealth-2016.ashx?la=en

[13] http://www.strokebestpractices.ca/index.php/news-feature/stroke-report-2016-just-released/

If Money Could Talk

help you recover your financial footing if you're not prepared for the setback of a critical illness.

Critical Illness Insurance

Critical Illness Insurance provides you with a living benefit to give you time and money to recover fully from a critical illness — comfortably, at your own pace, and without financial worries or lifestyle compromises. The way these policies work is that if you survive your illness for at least 30 days, you'll receive a lump sum of cash to spend as you see fit.

Of course, there are some strings attached to the coverage:

- A heart attack has to be deemed 'eligible' by the insurance company;

- There are special conditions for prostate cancer and breast cancer that you need to read closely in your policy.

Pick Your Poison

In addition, to the Big Three, the following conditions are insured in most Critical Illness policies, depending on which insurance company you choose

Multiple Sclerosis	Kidney Failure
Parkinson's Disease	Paralysis/Paraplegia
Major Organ Transplant	Severe Burns
Aorta Graft Surgery	Balloon Angioplasty
Benign Brain Tumour	Blindness in both eyes
Coma	Coronary Artery Disease
Heart Value Surgery	HIV / Blood Transfusion
Alzheimer's	HIV Medical Profession
Loss of Hearing	HIV Assault with Needle
Loss of Independent Existence	Loss of Limb
Loss of Speech	Motor Neurone Disease

I have Disability Insurance — isn't that enough?

There are some fundamental differences between Critical Illness and Disability Insurance.

- Critical Illness benefits are paid as a tax-free lump sum (for example, $100,000 or $250,000). Disability Income benefits are paid as monthly income, for a set period of time (for example, 5 years, or until you are age 65);

- To qualify for a Critical Illness benefit, you must be diagnosed with a designated illness and survive a waiting period, usually 30 days. To qualify for Disability Income benefits, you must be unable to perform all or parts of your job due to an injury or illness.

In some cases you may be eligible for a Critical Illness benefit, but not Disability Income, and vice versa. It is important to know the difference between the two and understand what you are covered for.

Famous Last Words: "I'll take my chances…"

If you have been thinking that it's a chance you're willing to take, you might want to think again. Let's suppose at a minimum, your illness takes you (and maybe also your spouse or caregiver) out of commission for six months. You will not only have given up six months (times two) of earnings, you will have depleted your savings by six months. And what if your illness lingers and you run out of savings? Your next avenue of recourse is to dip into a line of credit against your house. And then, once that becomes tenuous, the RRSPs are the next line of attack. And as we've talked about in a previous chapter, in addition to the illness, the raid on your savings and borrowing against your house, you'll also face a 30% tax load on the money you withdraw from your RRSP.

I am no doctor, of course, but I also have a hunch that having the cushion of a Critical Illness policy can actually help boost the client's recovery, since a major financial worry doesn't befall the client at the same time as the major illness.

Another Way of Looking at it

Just like other types of insurance — for example home insurance — if you don't ever need to make a claim, you're the lucky one. There's been a lot of talk about the addition of riders — or optional benefits — to Critical Illness insurance policies. The main one is the Return of Premium rider. This rider provides a refund of premiums paid at a certain point in time if no claim is made, but it comes at a cost. Whether this extra cost is of value is up to you. An advisor can help weigh the pros and cons of this option against other potential uses for the extra dollars.

Some Critical Illness policies are also convertible to Long Term Care Insurance later in life.

Long Term Care Insurance

Traditionally, we have counted on the government to provide for our medical needs, but when it comes to long-term care, you can expect the following from our medical system:

- Long waits, up to three or four years;
- Outdated and overcrowded facilities;
- No choice of location;
- Reduced services; and
- An annual financial assessment, to determine the level of subsidy received.

Unless you have medically-trained family members who are willing and able to drop everything and tend to you around the clock, you could find your retirement savings liquidated in a few short years if you elect to pay for private home care or facility care. Consider the following:

- Home care costs about $30 per hour, and up to $50 per hour for some services;

- Even a government facility will cost you from $750 to $1500 per month, even after the subsidy;

- Private facilities range from $2500 to $7000+ per month! And don't forget, this is the cost per person, not per couple.

Long-term care insurance covers virtually all of the expenses of long-term care, either in your own home or in a facility, for periods ranging from a few years to lifetime coverage. If you are between the ages of 30 and 80, you can apply for coverage. Depending on the level of benefit you select, you can receive up to $300 per day — tax free.

Although only a handful of companies in Canada currently offer this coverage, we can expect that many more will make it available in the next few years.

There are two types of Long Term Care Insurance policies:

- One reimburses you for eligible expenses you incur on a given day, up to a pre-set maximum; and

- The other type of long term care insurance is the income-style plan, which is more flexible. It offers income when you require care. You don't need to prove you had expenses.

Long term care may include:

- Nursing care;

- Rehabilitation and therapy;

- Personal care (help with activities of daily living like dressing, eating and bathing);

- Homemaking services (meals, cleaning, laundry); and

- Supervision by another person.

If Money Could Talk

$traight Talk

No one needs to be cut down in their prime pre-retirement earning years. Look into it. After age 50, the risks we need to insure become far more specific. Cancer, heart attacks, early-onset Alzheimers — just to name a few.

In my opinion, a Critical Illness policy can actually help boost your recovery, since a major financial worry won't befall you at the same time as a major illness.

Insurance providers are continually improving the benefits as the actuaries understand the odds. Policies continuously change. New types of insurance continue to arrive on the scene. If you haven't checked it out for a while, do so.

Your Relationship with Money

I see too many relationships destroyed by money. When you make the decision to live together as a couple, you not only share your home, you share your future and your finances.

The simple fact of it is that money means different things to different people. It can mean love, security, power or freedom. Vastly different attitudes toward money can cause unnecessary grief in your relationship, particularly when times get tough.

Most squabbles tend to be about saving vs. spending. A spender carries multiple credit cards, only pays the minimum amount and post-dates cheques so they won't bounce. These are all easy characteristics to spot even during the dating phase. A saver on the other hand, is the one who balances the chequing account every month, maxes the RRSP every year, always pays the credit card in full and keeps a separate account for emergencies. Most people fall somewhere in between.

Financial Infidelity

As a financial advisor, some of my clients treat me almost like a priest, confessing things to me that they've never confessed to their spouse. Usually it's just small stuff. They buy things they don't tell their partner about like clothing or beauty and personal care treatments, or food and restaurant meals. Those kinds of secrets don't seem to be really that big a deal if the partner simply isn't interested in the discussion and it's within the discretionary spending they've allowed each other.

So I wasn't entirely surprised to come across an American study[14] that showed married couples keep secrets about money more than anything else.

On a scale where independent spending is on the left and flamboyant infidelity is on the right, perhaps the most shocking stat I saw in the study is that 19% of Americans have a separate (and secret) credit card from their spouse. (Where do they send the bill? How do they pay for it without the partner finding out? Just how far do they go to keep it hidden?) If the same holds true in Canada, this means that when you look around your office today, one in five of your coworkers has a secret credit card. I'm baffled.

Captain and Crew

I often discover that by the time my clients hit 50, one has become the 'captain' and the other has been designated as 'crew' when it comes to managing the household's money. Even if you plan to both live until age 100, now is an important time to start sharing responsibility for managing money. That way, both of you will have control over your future and both will have the knowledge to deal with money if the other becomes ill. If you don't plan for

Equal Opportunity

I know it may sound old fashioned, but in the 21st century it still must be said: Both partners must have accounts registered in their own names. I still meet widows who find themselves without a credit card and without a credit rating, which makes it nigh-on impossible to live in this day and age.

❖

this possibility, the healthier spouse will be left alone to cope with this job at an already stressful time.

14 CESI Debt Solutions, 2010

But as we mature, it's also important to consider individual attitudes towards risk.

Choose Your Risks Wisely

Risk is a part of life. Of course, there are some risks that we can be comfortable with, some we can ignore and some we can manage. Most people get past the day-to-day risks, but many others get blind-sided by risks they didn't recognize. The same applies to financial risk. There are risks associated with having money, saving money, growing money and spending money. Simply put, once you understand the risks, you can take steps to manage and overcome them. So, here we go:

Risk of losing it.

Fear of losing the money we started with is what plagues most of us. There are all kinds of investments that promise great returns but the greater the return you expect or anticipate, the greater the risk that you will lose it all.

Risk of declining value.

If you're afraid of losing it, you might be tempted to keep your money under a mattress. But unless the money is growing, it is shrinking. Why? Inflation. A dollar stuffed under the mattress in 1990 has only two thirds of the purchasing power it had when it was socked away, so simply hoarding the cash has a risk all its own.

Risk of fluctuation.

If you've chosen an investment that has potential for going up, it also has potential for going down. And up and down. And up and down. That's known as volatility. If you're going to need the money in a short time frame or on a precise date, you want to be sure that on the date you need it, it's up and not down.

Risk of marketability.

For some types of investments such as real estate, art, collectables, etc., there is also a 'liquidity risk' which simply means that when you're ready to sell it, there may not be a buyer at hand who is willing to pay what you think it's worth.

Those are the big four risks, but guess what, there are more.

- **Risk of currency exchange**. Fluctuating exchange rates can cut into your return on investments made in foreign markets;

- **Economic risks.** Certain industries are very sensitive to fluctuations in the economy. The auto industry tends to do well in good times. Others, including utilities are less sensitive to economic cycles;

- **Industry risk.** With the rapid pace of technological change, some industries, such as the technology industry, are inherently volatile. Just ask anyone who had Nortel stocks;

- **Company risk.** When you own a stock, you own part of a business and even businesses in booming industries can be poorly managed. Think no further than Enron or Tyco;

- **Credit risk.** If you're buying bonds, you're lending money to a company or government. Interest payments could be suspended or you may not be repaid your principal if the borrower runs into financial difficulty;

- **Political risk.** If you're investing in foreign markets particularly, governments can and do change the rules.

So clearly, no matter what you invest in or whether you invest at all, your money is subject to risk. And if sleeping at night really is a worry, nothing beats having an advisor to help you figure out just how much risk you can handle, as well as recommend a portfolio that won't contain any surprises. The important part is to take your read of the situation, step off the bag, and make a commitment to run for second base.

The Quest for Rate of Return

So the opposite of the risk-averse, safety-minded investor is the jack-doodle who's always ready to brag about their latest stock market conquest. If you could picture a hamster wheel, this guy is on it and spinning faster and faster, but going nowhere fast. In actual fact, he's his own worst enemy and here's the ammo you need to nip the discussion in the bud:

- If you trade too often, you're running up costs. Commissions, taxes and poor market timing can suck the life out of any returns he might garner. I'm pretty sure he's never going to brag about that side of the deal.

- You're at an extreme disadvantage trading against big institutions. It's like deciding to play one-on-one with a professional basketball player. You're going to lose.

- You're much more likely to buy stocks that are among the 10% of stocks that are in the news — and to ignore the 90% of stocks that aren't but may offer greater value. Trust me, by the time it makes the news, the gains have already been had by those who arrived before you.

- Online trading has made it easier, but it hasn't improved the odds. The ease of online trading allows investors to follow their worst instincts. Just because it's easy, doesn't make it a good decision.

The opposite approach (think turtle vs. hare) is far more profitable both short and long term. Investing in a company because it has a great product, a great business model and a great management track record will go a lot further in your portfolio than a hot tip from the guy in the gym locker room. Holding onto it for as long as those factors hold) is the secret to success. It's never very exciting cocktail chatter, but the bragging rights will be all yours in due time.

Tune Out the Noise

In all of my years as a financial advisor, I can't count the number of times I've come across a mess that started out with bad advice. Advice from friends, family, the internet or television should always be treated as an idea to look into, but not necessarily take action on before you've checked with a professional advisor. And by professional advisor, I also mean an advisor who specializes in that kind of advice. You shouldn't get tax advice from a divorce lawyer and you shouldn't get legal advice from an accountant. The extra time and energy you invest in getting the right solution for your situation can save you and your family boatloads of trouble down the road. It's your money. It's your future. And it's worth the investment of time and attention of a pro.

Money in Your Home

While most of us have not yet reached the epidemic state of the poor souls who are featured on the TLC show *Hoarders: Buried Alive,* most of us do tend to collect a little too much stuff. There's an old adage that "stuff expands to fill the storage space available". And for some of us, when that limit is breached, we go out and purchase more storage space, rather than do the dastardly deed of pruning the stuff back.

Paper is one of the worst culprits that seems to mysteriously multiply — and every day the letter carrier seems to bring more! In fact, each time we go to the store, attend a class or pick up a newspaper the paper seems to grow.

But just how long do you need to keep all that stuff? Having seen more than my share of shoe-box filing systems, here is a handy reference that you can use for dealing with your home paper trail. (These rules don't apply if you're running a business from home! Totally different story.)

The stuff in your purse / wallet.

ATM and bank slips, once you've reconciled your account online or to your statement, can be tossed. Toss out receipts for meals, groceries, haircuts, personal services, movie tickets, parking stubs — stuff that you can't return. Once you've accounted for the expense in your cheque register / budget — let it go!

Credit card receipts.

If there's a chance you'll need to return it or use it as a proof of purchase, keep it until your monthly statement comes. If it's for a major purchase (bicycles, artwork, jewelry) keep it as a proof of purchase — especially if the value is higher than your insurance deductible. If it has a warranty, (appliances, etc.), staple the receipt to the owner's manual and file it.

Sign of the Times

When you're tossing your financial records, make sure you shred them and DO NOT put them in the general trash or recycling to avoid any chance of identity theft.

❖

Bank statements.

Most (all?) banks now offer paperless statements if you're banking online. It's a great way to keep the paper out of the house in the first place! It's also not likely that many banks are still offering to return your cancelled cheques — that's another service that really has gone the way of the dodo bird. If you're still getting cancelled cheques, stop them! If you're using a paperless statement, a digital image of your cheque is probably available online for free in case you really need to see it. Even if you're still getting paper statements, 12 months on a rolling basis is likely the most you'll ever need to have on file.

Brokerage statements / Investments.

These usually come on either a monthly or quarterly basis. And again, most institutions offer an option to go paperless if you have online access. If you receive an annual statement, the monthly or quarterly statements can be tossed once you receive the annual statement (it contains the same information, but in fewer pages). If you make trades or transactions throughout the year, the confirmations you receive can be thrown away as soon as you receive the next statement (they're like bank ATM slips).

Order in the House

Although I've come across many unusual filing systems, the best idea is to set up a simple home filing system to cover the basics, and invest in a couple of sturdy cardboard or plastic filing boxes for the information you should keep long-term or indefinitely.

❖

Utility bills.

Most utilities are using epost™ or have built their own online system for distribution of monthly bills, so if you're still receiving a paper version, check into the availability of an online alternative. There's no need to print online invoices (just store them online in a file folder) unless you need a printed copy for some purpose other than your love of filing. Whether you're storing paper or online, a 12-month rolling system is always adequate—when you add a new one, toss out or delete the oldest.

Pay stubs.

Once you've received your tax form, these can be shredded.

Real estate.

Records and supporting documents for acquisitions and disposal of property—especially those that would have an impact upon sale or liquidation must be kept indefinitely. To that end, you might want to keep records and receipts for major home

---

™ Trademark of Canada Post

improvements/renovations and receipts for major purchases that might be sold along with the house such as a new air conditioner, furnace, swimming pool, etc.

So after you've done a good pruning of the financial detritus that has been cluttering up your desk and filing cabinet, what do you need to keep?

- Home and Life Insurance policy information should be kept on file for as long as the policy is in force. Be sure to throw out last year's policy when you file this year's;

- Automobile Repairs — keep for as long as you own your vehicle to increase the value of your resale;

- Adoption Records, Birth Certificates and Social Insurance Numbers, Death Certificate;

- Marriage Certificate (or Divorce Agreement and/or Child Custody Court Orders);

- Degrees and Diplomas and in some cases final transcripts;

- Wills, Powers of Attorney, Health Care Directives should be kept securely in a fire-proof home safe or safety deposit box at your financial institution, or else on file at your executor's office.

Memorabilia, mementos and keepsakes

If you were told tomorrow that you have a few months to live, what would truly be important to your heirs and successors among your memorabilia, mementos and keepsakes? Your kindergarten report cards? Your participation certificate from sixth grade? Your diary as a pre-teen? Your teenage poetry? Photos of your university frat days? Your college text books? Your university notes? Ticket stubs from that Clapton concert in 1997? Sure they're things that were a part of your life. But if you're sharing your workspace with piles of paper, these are things you might actually agree can be parted with. It's the memories that count — not the papers.

$traight Talk

Don't let money ruin your relationship. Honesty and open discussion can ward off a lot of evil.

Risk is a part of life. Accept it. Embrace it. Taxes and fees are a part of life too.

Get your advice from a pro, not from the internet, television or friends and family.

Choosing a Financial Advisor Isn't Easy

Why? Financial product advertising ranges from absolutely boring to the blatantly overstated. Often the cost of doing business or even client service can be misleading or confusing. How do you feel when you read or hear about an investment that claims to offer huge returns? Have you ever experienced high pressure sales tactics? Although the majority of financial advisors are honest in their daily dealings, there are still some who are either unqualified or filled with worthless and hurtful advice. Many of these who are out to intentionally 'rip off' the public for their own benefit are eventually caught; however, at that point it is of little comfort to those who have had their life savings liquidated. How can you hope to find a qualified, competent, professional, honest and creditable advisor?

The promises and pitfalls

"No fees" and "low fees"

Chances are the person who says this is likely a commission-based advisor. There is a difference between "commissions" and "fees." While the "no fees" statement is essentially true, it is also deceptive. There is a cost of doing business with an advisor whether you can see fees and charges up front or not. Remember: you never get 'something' for 'nothing' and there's no free lunch. Find out all costs you are expected to be charged and get it in writing before you sign on the dotted line.

"Low fees"

Even a claim of 'low fees' can be deceptive because the fee that is being advertised is likely not what you will pay, especially if the advisor is using products that have built-in fees, like mutual funds. You may think you are paying the lowest price, but, in fact, you may end up paying the highest fees and not even know it.

Understanding exactly how your advisor is compensated is very important. Consider this: if your advisor only receives a commission whenever they buy or sell a stock, bond or mutual fund in your account, how much can you trust their recommendations? If they are paid by fees only, you'll need to understand what the fee is and how they charge it.

Commissions are not wrong—neither are fees. Once you understand how your advisor gets paid for certain products and services, you can then ask why something is being recommended. Knowing how your advisor gets paid will help you tremendously. If your current advisor or an advisor you are considering hiring does not want to clearly answer questions about their compensation, that could be a sign they are trying to hide something. It may be an indication that they are not thinking of your best interest, but possibly of their own.

If you pick an advisor because you think their fee is the lowest and it ends up costing you tons more in overpaid taxes, what is the point?

An advisor that is commission-only works on the

Qualifying Questions to Ask

1) Do you work as a fiduciary?

2) How are you registered with provincial and federal securities regulators?

3) How long have you been an advisor?

4) What are your credentials?

5) How do you get paid for different investments or account types?

6) What is your investment philosophy?

❖

rule of suitability – not on a fiduciary basis.

Bait and switch

Whenever you read an advertisement that quotes a high interest rate in a low interest rate environment, beware. Some financial institutions have "teaser" rates. These interest rates are only good for a short time—their only purpose is to acquire new clients. The institution will pay you this extra interest and consider it an advertising cost to them. The goal is to then sell you a bundle of products that is highly profitable (to them, not you). Many investors are tricked into moving their money thinking they will always earn a higher interest rate than they are currently getting. Don't fall for it. Read the details of any offer and ask questions.

Outrageous claims

Be very cautious of advertised high rates of return — especially "guaranteed" ones. Get the details in writing and don't make any snap decisions. If the advisor hesitates or claims there is nothing available in writing, you need to walk away. If something sounds too good to be true, it most likely is.

House calls

If an advisor is coming to your house, make sure it's because they are offering you a special service, not because they don't have an office! If you go to their office and it is in one of those rent-by-the-hour offices that is not good either. Many start-up advisors are part of a "bullpen" where they sit in a large room of desks with phones and guest workstations. That's not a bad thing, but it's definitely a testament to their experience level.

You can tell a lot about an advisor and their operation by visiting their office. You can see if they have support staff and you can get a good feel if they are successful or not. I recommend that one of the first things you do is visit the advisor's office and check them out thoroughly.

The first appointment

If you meet an advisor who tries to get you to sign up on the first appointment, get up and leave and never talk to them again. You don't want to rush into anything when you are seeking a long-term relationship. If they are offering solutions on the first appointment, do you believe they are doing their own due diligence about you? Are they analyzing your situation and trying to come up with the best solution? Or are they simply trying to sell you something?

The "too good to be true" story

It is very tempting to believe the "too good to be true" story. Why? Because you wish there was really something that could be that good. It would make your life easier. Something that sounds "too good" is almost always not true. Don't believe the hype.

Outdated beliefs

In the 'old days', Canada's financial system had four distinct pillars that had very clear roles and purposes in our lives.

- Banks were allowed to sell deposit accounts and lend money

- Insurance companies were allowed to sell all kinds of insurance products

- Securities firms were allowed to sell stocks, bonds, mutual funds etc.

- Trusts companies were able to act as trustees such as in bankruptcy and estate matters.

Times have changed and so has the industry. Banks offer brokerage and insurance, insurance companies offer mortgages, and brokers offer banking products. All offer similar types of advice—with all levels of experience, qualifications and access to all kinds of products. You cannot assume that a broker has more experience than a banker, or that an insurance representative has fewer products to offer than a broker. It all comes down to finding the right person, with experience and qualifications that match your needs, your personality and your situation.

Fancy titles

Along with the commingling of the products and services offered by financial institutions, their advisors also have similar titles. You'll hear insurance agents, stock brokers, banking reps, mutual fund sales people and others employed in the financial services industry use the title "financial representative," or "financial advisor". Other than in Quebec, these titles don't reflect experience or qualifications, they merely imply that the individual has passed a licensing requirement to sell products.

Depending on your needs, you will want an advisor with experience in areas of specialty that will benefit you. The skills needed to advise a person in or near retirement are much different than the skills needed to advise someone who is just starting out at their first job.

Bigger company ≠ better advice

As Canadians, we place a great deal of trust in our banking system. And while we're all very grateful for its size and stability, it doesn't necessarily mean that banks can offer better advice. In fact, you may be more likely to be working with a rookie because many financial advisors begin their career and get their training at some of the largest institutions around, like a bank. As an advisor gains experience and a loyal customer base, they often choose to work independently. Why? Many times, it is so they can service client needs better. By being independent, the advisor can offer a world of options and solutions to clients. Other times they leave the larger firms because they do not like being obligated to sell proprietary products. An independent advisor or one that works in a non-restrictive sales environment can put your interest first.

Doing it yourself

You may feel you can do just as good a job on your own. You may be right. But a competent advisor lives, eats, and breathes financial topics all day, every day. Do you really want to do that in your golden years? Most who do it themselves really don't want to, but feel that they have to. They may feel they can't afford an advisor. However, is the stress and uncertainty worth it? Having the right advisor does not eliminate your position as CEO of your life. You are just hiring a CFO to assist you.

Agency. Fiduciary. Broker.

There is a big difference between a financial advisor who works as an "agent", one who works as a "fiduciary" and one who works as a "broker".

Agency

Agency relationships are used extensively in business. In the financial industry, the law of agency is what gives advisors and their firms the ability to enter trades on behalf of the client without the client being in direct contact with the party on the other side of the trade. It is also what allows a client to give trading authority over his or her account to a third party, through either a Trading Authorization form, or, more formally, a Power of Attorney. With a properly signed account agreement, advisors do not require written instructions from clients every time an order is placed. The law recognizes that the advisor has authority to proceed to do what is customary in his or her business in carrying out the instructions.

Fiduciary

The Fiduciary is a person who holds a position of trust and has a duty to the individual who has placed trust in that person. This could be in connection with the care of assets or when they are responsible for the personal affairs of others. Fiduciary duties have been found to exist in relationships such as: doctor/patient, lawyer/client, and director/corporation.

Historically, courts have found that a financial advisor may owe a fiduciary duty to a client if the advisor provided investment advice and the client relied on such advice. The existence of a fiduciary relationship imposes the highest standard of care— honesty, good faith—on the advisor.

Broker

The relationship of an investor to his or her investment banker or broker will not likely give rise to a fiduciary duty of that broker as the broker is simply a conduit of information and an order taker.

Alphabet Soup? The Importance of Credentials

Financial Analyst, Financial Advisor, Financial Consultant, Financial Planner, Investment Consultant or Wealth Manager are generic terms or job titles. They may be used by investment employees (or independents) who do not hold any specific designation. It is important to research credentials so you know what it took to earn it. Listed below are a few common and legitimate designations in Canada:

Certified Financial Planner (CFP®)

One of the most widely known designations is the CFP or Certified Financial Planner offered by the Financial Planning Standards Council. To obtain the CFP designation, candidates must complete a rigorous education program, pass two national exams and have three years of qualifying work experience. To maintain certification, every year they complete new professional education courses and agree to adhere to a set of standards for professional responsibility.

There is a national registry of CFPs at www.fpsc.ca.

Personal Financial Planner (PFP®)

The PFP is a similar designation to the CFP. It was developed by the banking industry about 20 years ago, but was eventually taken over by the Canadian Securities Institute.

Chartered Investment Manager (CIM®)

The CIM is offered by the Canadian Securities Institute and focuses on discretionary portfolio management services and high level strategies tailored to affluent clients. To take the course, the advisor must have at least two years' experience in an investment management capacity that includes applying or supervising any aspect of the investment management process or providing expert analysis or evaluation in support of the investment management process.

Chartered Strategic Wealth Professional (CSWP)

Another designation offered by the Canadian Securities Institute, the designation requires a preexisting designation such as PFP, CFP, CLE or FMA and three different programs in the designation:

- Advanced Retirement Management Strategies and a certificate in Retirement Strategy

- Advanced Investment Strategies and a certificate in Advanced Investment Advice

- Advanced Estate Planning and Trust Strategies, leading to the Certficiate in Estate Planning & Trust Strategy

Fellow of CSI (FCSI®)

Also a designation by the Canadian Securities Institute, a Fellow of CSI is a designation that includes a combination of at least 7 years' experience and at least one of a number of advanced designations such as PFP, CIWM, CIM, CFP , etc.

$traight Talk

You never get 'something' for 'nothing' and there's no free lunch. If you are interviewing a new advisor, make sure you ask about their compensation up front. Remember, quality has a price.

The skills needed to advise a person in or near retirement are much different than the skills needed to advise someone who is just starting out at their first job.

Regardless of what type of firm you are working with, it's important to enter a fiduciary relationship.

Don't Worry. Be Happy.

When people worry, they don't eat well, they exercise less, and they generally don't maintain a healthy sleep schedule.

My goal for all of my clients is to make sure that money is not keeping them awake at night. With all of the stresses that can be foisted upon adults in their 50s, financial stress is one that can be easily beaten by connecting with a professional who keeps on top of the financial environment and can help you make sense of what's going on in your life from an investment, tax, estate, insurance or retirement perspective.

If you had to give peace of mind a monetary value, what would it be? Many would say it is priceless. The more stress we have, the quicker we age, the worse our health becomes and the more tired we become. Peace of mind allows us to relax and pay attention to the really important areas of our life. We can focus on family, friends and health and reach some of the goals we have longed to accomplish our whole life. There is no joy when one has to worry about where the money will come from to pay the bills.

No matter how much you have, you will always worry unless you have sound planning. Without proper planning, there is an underlying worry that will eat away at you. A little nagging voice inside of you that says, "You better look into this."

Financial peace of mind does not come from having more than you can ever spend. It comes from having enough to do things you desire. It is knowing that you have a plan in place to take care of the basics and, if circumstances allow, the 'fun' things you always wanted to do.

A final few words... Don't procrastinate! Get it done now. If you don't have a plan, get one right away. If the plan you have is one you made a while ago, get it updated. Just like a will, you should update your financial plan every time there is a significant change in your life – and retiring, or getting close to it, is one of those times.

Index

Retirement. It Takes Practice. 1

The Wild Card 1

Retirement Syndrome 3

Replacing Your Purpose 4

A Door Closes. A Door Opens. 5

The Other Big Questions 5

Where will you live? 5

How will you spend your time? 6

What big obligations do you have? 6

Got the Travel Bug? 6

Be Careful What You Ask For 7

Advertising vs Reality 7

So How Much Do You Need? 9

The go-go phase. 9

Do You Still Need a Cushion? 10

The slow-go phase. 10

The no-go phase. 11

Spending Your Way to Happiness 13

Know Your Numbers 13

What is an hour of your time really worth? 13

What does it take to run the ship? 13

If you don't like what you learn, make adjustments. 14

Good Debts vs Bad Debts 14

Money in Your Wallet 15

Funding Your Mid-Life Crisis 17

Money Has No Feelings 17

Borrowing to boost your RRSP 18

How a $21,000 Spending Spree Costs $72,000 19

Hands Off that Tax Refund 19

Free Up Short-Term Cash 19

Free Up Future Cash 20

Pay Yourself Forward 20

Pay It Forward For Others... 21

Spending Spree 21

Taking Care of Business.. 23

Life After Work... 23

Are you ready to sell?... 24

The Cost of Life on the Outside.. 25

Ready to Hand Over the Baton?.. 25

What's Your Business Worth? 26

Prepare Your Business for Sale 26

First, get your books in order... 27

Be ready to dig for paperwork.. 27

Spruce it up... 27

Never as Easy as it Looks 27

Seller's Remorse... 28

Notes for the Family Enterprise.. 28

All Things Considered 29

Do NOT Try This At Home.. 30

No Place For Emotions 31

Stay Flexible, My Friend 31

Filling Your Retirement Bucket 33

Government Benefits 33

Canada/Quebec Pension Plan (CPP/QPP).................................34

Old Age Security (OAS). 34

Guaranteed Income Supplement (GIS). 34

Pension Plans 34

Defined Benefit (DB) Plans...34

Defined Contribution (DC) Plans. 35

A Personal Pension Plan. 35

RRSPs — Where the Rubber Meets the Road.........................35

Shell-shocked investing...35

Paying too much tax on the outside. 35

Getting fancy. 36

Squirreling. 36

Missing opportunities..36

Not naming a beneficiary..36

Other Personal Assets 36

Tax Free Savings Accounts (TFSAs). 37

Annuities..38

Covering the Bases..39

One tickbox can change your life.. 41

Another Box to Tick..42

On Early Retirement..43

The Golden Handshake..45

Did You Get A Fair Deal? 45

Deer in the Headlights? 46

Roll it into an RRSP. 46

Spread the severance over calendar years..........................46

Make up your unused RRSP contributions. 46

What Now?...47

Are You Ready To Check Out? 47

The Bucket System for Retirement 49

  Take the Fear Out of Spending 49

  Managing the Big Bucket 51

  Managing the Markets 52

  Eggs in Baskets 53

Your Home is Your Castle 55

  Tapping into your Home 55

    But here's the flip side of the coin. 55

  A Better Solution 56

  Life Lease 57

A Blizzard for Snowbirds 59

  The IRS has You in its Sights 60

  A substantial presence 60

  Owning US Property 61

    A 30% flat tax. 61

    Rental expenses. 61

    CRA's share. 62

  A Non-Resident Tax Return 62

  US Taxes at Death 62

  The Trick is Not to Die Before... 63

  About Timeshares 63

'Til Death Do Us Part 65

  The Four Biggest Fears 65

    Fear of facing mortality. 65

    Fear of stirring up old family conflicts. 65

    Fear of creating new family conflicts. 66

    Fear of losing control. 66

  Tips for 'The Talk' 66

    Will. 67

Executor. 67

Bequests. 68

Eldercare. 68

Tax Planning. 68

Health Care Directives. 68

Power of Attorney. 68

Funeral wishes. 69

Axes, Exes and Revenge 69

Choosing An Executor 70

So Now You Tell Me 72

Trusts 72

On Your Own 74

How To Screw Up Your Estate Plan With One Signature 76

Trying to Avoid Probate 76

Joint Ownership 76

Beneficiary Designations 77

'Til Divorce Do Us Part 81

Your home. 81

Your spouse and children. 81

Children are Not a Weapon 82

Division of Property 82

Division of Debts 84

Tax Issues in Divorce 85

Retirement Plan Issues in Divorce 85

A Word About Dishonest Spouses 85

Questionable transactions and other sleights of hand 86

Picking Up the Pieces 86

It Takes Time 87

Dependent Adults 89

Tax Planning 90

Estate Planning 91

Beware of the Inheritance Trap 92

A Quick 5-Pack on the RDSP 93

Your Executor Holds the Key 93

Committeeships 94

Lifetime Benefit Trust 95

Trusts 96

Insurance 96

The Peanut Butter Generation 99

Stuck in the middle with you 99

A Few Words on the Funeral Industry 100

Embalming is not required by law. 101

Cremation. 102

Casket Capers. 103

Leaving a Legacy 105

Holograph Wills 106

Drugstore Wills 106

Who Cares. I'll be Dead. 107

And Furthermore 108

Life Insurance After Age 50? 109

Final Expense Policies. 110

Guaranteed Issue. 110

Business Insurance. 111

Other Reasons. 111

Mortgage Insurance 111

Accidental-Death Insurance 113

6 Ways to Leave a Legacy 113

Gift through a will. 113